Seminole & Creek War Chronology

Dade's Battle, from Moore's <u>Indian Wars of the United States</u>, 1858.

By Christopher Delano Kimball
©2013

2015 reprint & edit
This edition is essentially the same as the previous, except that I have increase the font size. I am growing old & feeble, and the tiny print was getting hard to read!

Bob Davis
Thank You!
Christopher Kimball

Dedication

To my parents who help encourage me to follow my dream.

Acknowledgements

I need to thank many people who encouraged and helped me along the way the past twenty years. Some must remain unanimous for reasons we both understand. To my friends and helpful research coaches: Dr. Joe Knetsch, and John & Mary Lou Missall. To my Seminole / Miccosukee friend on Brighton Reservation who was grandmother to everyone and an amazing woman; I miss her since her journey across the Milky Way. To the elders and keepers of the traditions who know me well and have steered me in the right direction; you know who you are. To the fat nasty bastard (I say that in friendship) who helped teach me 19th century soldiering at Fort Morgan. To Kent Low who keeps history alive. To Steve Abolt, one of the best living history interpreters I know. To Earl DeBary who was my partner in crime & research. To friends in scouting Rick Obermeyer and Jimmy Sawgrass.

Contents

Chapter:	Page:
Introduction	1
Bloody Alachua During the 2nd Seminole War (Map)	7
Part 1 1513-1699: The Spanish Change Florida Forever	12
Part 2 1700-1799: Seminoles Settle in Florida	16
Part 3 1800-1815: Invasion & War in the Southeast	22
Part 4 1816-1818: The First Seminole War	34
Part 5 1819-1834: Treaties Written, Treaties Broken	39
Part 6 1835: Crisis as War Begins Again	48

Part 7   54
1836: Seminoles Claim the First
Victories and Another Creek Uprising

Part 8   69
1837: Betrayal and Defeat

Part 9   79
1838: Retreat to the Everglades

Part 10   83
1839-1840: The Bloody War of Attrition

Part 11   93
1841: Unending Campaign Against the
Seminoles

Part 12   97
1842: The End of the War

Part 13   100
1842-1855: An Uneasy Truce

Part 14   103
1855-1858: The Third Seminole War

Bibliography   110

Introduction

*"Austere remembrance of the deed will hang
Upon its delicate spirit like a cloud,
And tinge its world of happy images
With hues of horror."*

"The Florida war consisted in the killing of Indians, because they refused to leave their native home -- to hunt them amid the forests and swamps, from which they frequently issued to attack the intruders. To go or not to go, that was the question."

"Many a brave man lost his life and now sleeps beneath the sod of Florida. And yet neither these nor the heroes who exposed themselves there to so many dangers and sufferings, could acquire any military glory in such a war."

(From "The Army and Navy of America," by Jacob K. Neff, Philadelphia, J.H. Pearsol & Co., 1845.)

Let us not forget!

We should not forget these people who have died on both sides!

Participating in living history events for the Second Seminole War, it became obvious that most people in Florida are not aware of the state's rich history or unique culture of the Seminoles. The longest and most costly war the United States ever fought against any Native American Indian tribe was right here, and there are not many reminders that it ever happened. Most people have no idea where to look for information even if they want to know more. Sadly, travelling around the state, you will not find many places that commemorate this war.

Due to scattered sources of information, I began to compile a list of all the battles and skirmishes of the three Florida or Seminole wars, including the two Creek wars as well. During my effort, I found out information on several bloody battles that seemed to have been completely forgotten.

I was pretty much finished by 2001 (or so I thought) and printed a small number of booklets at a local print shop. If you are one of the few who have an earlier copy of that book, you may recognize this as very similar to the earlier humble printing.

The War of 1812 bicentennial is here, which is also the bicentennial of the first Creek War. Since a lot of new material has been published about the two Creek wars recently, I have added a lot more information on them as well. I now feel confident that I have the best listing of battles and events of the combined Creek and Seminole wars that anyone has ever compiled.

If I am off a day or two of the actual events, it is unintentional. When I have found conflicting dates from different sources, I hopefully chose the best one. Sources can be regrettably flawed.

What Do You Call These Folks?

People are often confused about the difference between Seminoles, Miccosukees, and Creeks. They all have mostly the same cultural beliefs and practices. And many written sources make it confusing as well. There are people who are called both Seminole or Miccosukee during the 2nd Seminole War. During the 2nd Creek War, the group of Creeks in revolt were called Seminoles. These are from the writings of those times. In the 1940s or 1950s, there were people along the Tamiami Trail in South Florida who were called Seminoles, but after the Miccosukee Tribe received federal recognition in 1962, they were called Miccosukee. Spelling in various sources differ, so you will see different spellings throughout this text.

It is very difficult from using the historical sources to always determine the identity of an unidentified tribe or group. Although I use Seminole to identify the Indians, it is often used in the general sense, even if the Indians might be Miccosukee, or even Creek. There's precedence for this generalization in the historic record. A letter written by Indian Agent Wiley Thompson in 1835 explains why all the Indians in Florida are referred to as

Seminoles, even if they are Muskogee, Miccosukee, Yuchi, or others. At that time, Thompson considered all the Indians in Florida as Seminoles, no matter what their origin.

> "The word Seminole means runaway or broken off. Hence Seminole is a distinctive appellation, applicable to all the Indians in the Territory of Florida, as all of them run away, or broke off, from the Creek or Nuiscoge [Muskogee] nation. The treaties made with the Seminole Indians embrace all the Indians within the Territory, except some bands on the Apalachicola river, who were provided for by a separate article in the Camp Moultrie treaty; and, subsequently, by treaties entered into immediately between these bands and the United States." (<u>U.S. Congress (24th Congress, 2d Session), January 23, 1837; Report from the Secretary of War, In Compliance with Resolution of the Senate of the 14th and 18th Instant, Transmitting Copies of Correspondence Relative to the Campaign in Florida.</u>)

Later, the groups of Indians hostile towards removal and who fought against the United States are many times said to be Miccosukee. The groups that surrendered to the United States and waited in Tampa for deportation are called Seminoles. Osceola is called both Seminole and Miccosukee. Actually, Osceola was neither;

he was originally a Tallassee Creek from Alabama. But in practice, everyone recognizes Osceola as the most famous Seminole in history. Confused yet?

The Seminole and Miccosukee people themselves will tell many stories of their origins, depending on family and clan differences. One Seminole lady told me that her ancestors were from northern Georgia, of one of the great Mississippian mound builder cities. Some of my Miccosukee neighbors tell me that they have ancestors among the Calusa. Reading John Swanton's many works on the various Creek towns, it is obvious that the Creek ancestors are from many people who joined together. But one thing remains undisputed: the current Seminole and Miccosukee people in Florida are the descendants of the great Mound Builders and continue that legacy.

Much has been written about the Black Seminoles. I do not like to use the term "African American," because the Black Seminoles were neither African, nor American. They were more Spanish, or Seminole. If the term Negro is used, it is taken directly from the historical record and is not intended in a derogatory manner or to offend anyone.

When I mention Army, it can mean either the regular army or the different state and volunteer militias. Ever since the creation of the United States, a large national army was distrusted. The majority of the defense of the country was left to the citizens who would muster together in times of crises and defend their homes. But the Second Seminole War made it necessary to create more regiments in the national Army and increase the number of soldiers. The fighting overwhelmed the citizens of Florida, and soon help was sought among other states for their volunteer militia regiments to join in the fighting.

Bloody Alachua during the 2nd Seminole War

For those not familiar with Florida geography, here are some important sites in Florida during the 2nd Seminole War. Early into this research, I quickly learned that the most active area in the Florida War was Alachua County and the surroundings.

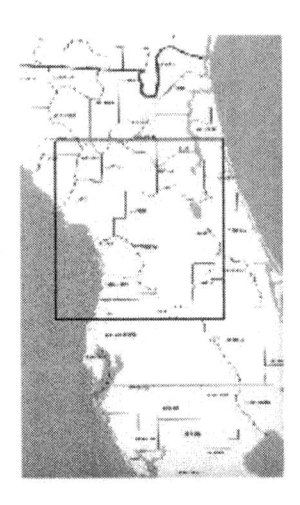

Map of North Central Florida. See the map on the following page for details of the area in the square.

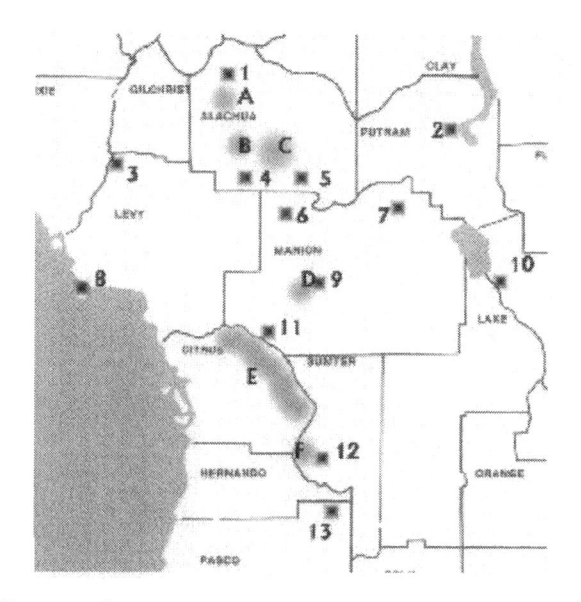

Legend:

- A: San Felasco Hammock -- Today a State Preserve. A large battle took place here on September 18, 1836 between the Indians and a large force of Florida Militia and Regular Army Troops.
- B: Kanapaha Prairie -- An extension of Alachua (Paynes) prairie. Several bloody battles were fought in the area, including the Battle of Black Point on December 18, 1835; which was the prelude to the Second Seminole War when Florida Militia forces were attacked and driven off by Seminoles.
- C: Alachua (Paynes) Prairie -- Today known as Paynes Prairie State Preserve. Some of the early Seminole

in Florida moved into this area and had large herds of livestock. Cattle have been raised here since Spanish times.
- D: Big Swamp -- There were many Seminole villages here. Now underneath Ocala city streets and houses.
- E: The Cove of the Withlacoochee -- This was thought to be the hiding place of the main Seminole force in the beginning of the war. Four large campaigns under Generals Clinch, Gaines, Scott, and Governor Call failed to locate and drive out the Indians.
- F: Wahoo Swamp -- Major battle on November 21, 1836 with Seminoles fighting regular Army soldiers, state Militia, and the U.S. Creek Indian Regiment.
1. Newnansville -- Largest Florida inland town in the 1830's. It no longer exists.
2. Palatka -- Supply depot and major port on the St. Johns River.
3. Fort Fanning -- Crossing on the Suwannee River. Today known as Fanning Springs.
4. Fort Wacahoota -- Several bloody battles were fought in the area of this fort and along the road to Micanopy. Considered the bloodiest road in Florida.

5. Micanopy -- Town and Fort with the same name. Formerly site of Chief Micanopy's town. Osceola leads a major attack nearby on Fort Defiance on June 9, 1836.
6. Fort Drane -- General Clinch fortified his plantation and established this fort. Often under siege by the Seminoles. When the fort was abandoned in the summer of 1836, Seminoles under Osceola's leadership took up residence and used the abandoned grain stores.
7. Payne's Landing -- Treaty made here between the Seminoles and United States in 1832. Later the Seminoles would claim that they did not have good interpreters and did not understand what they were signing.
8. Cedar Key -- Major supply depot established by General Taylor in 1839.
9. Fort King -- One of the most important forts in Florida from 1827 to 1844. Main Indian Agency from 1825 to 1842. Today the City of Ocala.
10. Volusia -- Crossing on the St. Johns River. Being on a Spanish map of 1558 makes it one of the oldest European settlements.
11. Camp Izard -- Crossing on the Withlacoochee River where General Gaines and 1,200 men were trapped and surrounded by Indians for over

a week in early March 1836. Today part of state preserved land.
12. Dade's Battlefield – Considered the beginning of the Second Seminole War, it was the most costly battle to United States forces in Florida on December 28, 1835. Named after Major Dade, who was the first casualty. Of about 110 soldiers, only three survived. Privates Clark & Sprague, and slave Louis Pacheco.
13. Fort Dade -- Crossing on the Withlacoochee River. Dade City is now in this area. A cease fire agreement was made here between the Miccosukee and General Macomb, Commanding General of the Army, in May 1839.

Part 1

1513-1699: The Spanish Change Florida Forever

Before 1513 – The estimates of the original population of Florida Natives before the Spanish, range anywhere from 25,000 to 1 million. 250 years later, a small surviving remnant left with the Spanish for Cuba. Decimated by disease and slavery, they numbered only a few hundred.

Hontoon Island on the St. Johns River. Once a large village of Timuquan Indians. Photo by author.

2 April 1513 - Ponce de Leon first sights Florida and lands the next week somewhere between the mouth of the St. Johns River and Cape Canaveral. He claims Florida for the King of Spain and sails around the peninsula.

1521 - Ponce de Leon tries to establish a Spanish colony near Charlotte Harbor, but is mortally wounded in an attack by Calusa Indians.

4 or 15 April 1528 - Panfilo de Narvaez lands an exhibition of 400 soldiers in Tampa Bay to search for gold. It ends in failure with only four survivors who walk to Mexico City eight years later.

May 1528 - The Spanish force under Panfilo de Narvaez battles a large force of Native Floridians near the Withlacoochee River.

18 May 1539 - Hernando de Soto lands in search of gold in what is either Tampa Bay or Charlotte Harbor. He will travel all over the southeast and not survive himself.

26 June 1549 - Missionary Father Luis Cancer de Barbastro arrives in Tampa Bay to minister to the Indians, but is immediately clubbed to death.

11 June 1559 - Tristan de Luna y Arellano lands in Pensacola Bay but fails in his attempt to establish a colony after 22 months of hardships.

April 1561 - Angel de Villafane replaces de Luna, but also fails to establish a permanent colony in Pensacola.

30 April 1562 - French Huguenot Jean Ribault lands at the mouth of the St. Johns

River, plants a stone column claiming it for France, and moves up to what is now South Carolina and establishes Charles Fort. It is abandoned when food supplies run out.

22 June 1564 - Rene Goulaine de Laudonniere reestablishes the French presence by constructing Fort Caroline at the mouth of the St. Johns River.

28 June 1565 - Pedro Menendez de Aviles lands in Florida with a Spanish military exhibition to stop the French, and establishes the town of St. Augustine.

20 September 1565 - The Spanish surprise and overrun Fort Caroline, kill many of the French, and rename it Fort San Mateo.

Rebuilt Fort Caroline near Jacksonville. Photo by author.

10 October 1565 - Menendez kills most of the remaining French Huguenots including their leader Ribault.

26 November 1565 - Menendez finds a remaining group of French survivors shipwrecked near Cape Canaveral and sends them back to Spain as slaves. Spain now has firm control over Florida, with no real challenge for the next 135 years.

Part 2

1700-1799: Seminoles Settle in Florida

1702-1706 - English Governor James Moore from Charleston leads a series of raids into present day Georgia and Florida to enslave Indians, and destroys the Spanish mission chain. The English bring Yamassee Indian allies and kill many of the aboriginal Florida Indians.

After 1713 - After the Queen Anne's War of 1701-1713, Spain encourages Lower Creeks to settle in Florida as a buffer against the English.

1715 - The British turn against and defeat the Yamassees of South Carolina, who flee to St. Augustine and support the Spanish. A Creek/Yamassee combination becomes part of the early Seminoles.

1732 The English settle Georgia, increasing Creek migrations into Florida.

1739-50 - Pro-Spanish Chief Secoffee's band moves into the Apalachee area of northern Florida. Pro-English Cowkeeper's clan (Oconee/Mikasuki) moves into the Alachua region. The Creeks were divided by European powers seeking their support with trade contracts. Secoffee's group mixed with aboriginal Apalachicolas and became Seminoles. Mikasuki or Hitchiti speaking groups moved into west Florida during the same time.

13 June-4 July 1740 - General James Oglethorpe from the English Colony of Georgia surrounds and tries to take St. Augustine, but fails. With Oglethorpe is a large force of Creek, Chickasaw, and Uchize (Yuchi) Indians, who raid northern and central Florida.

The Author in early 19th Century Seminole clothing at a reenactment event at the Big Cypress Seminole Indian Reservation in February 1999.

27 February-30 March 1743 - General Oglethorpe again tries to take Florida and St. Augustine. Once again he fails and is forced to retreat. He brings a large force of Indians made up of Cherokee and Upper & Lower Creeks, who attack Yamassee that are friendly with the Spanish. This was the last time the British attempted to take Florida before it was ceded to them in 1763.

1750-1814 - Large migrations of Muskogean and Mikasuki Creeks from Georgia and Alabama move into Florida.

1763 - The British acquire Florida from Spain as part of the treaty ending the Seven Years War. The Spanish leave Florida with 500 of the last aboriginal Florida Indians. During the next 20 years an extensive trading system develops between the British and the Southeastern Indians, which stays in place even after Spain gets Florida back in 1783.

1767 - Muskogee speaking Eufaula Indians from Georgia move into the Tampa Bay area. Other Muskogees became the Tallahassees in the panhandle.

1773 - Famous botanist William Bartram surveys the St. Johns River and writes much about his visits with the Seminoles.

Around 1778 the British encourage more Hitchiti and Muskogee speaking bands to move into Florida.

1783 - The Spanish are given back Florida from the British as a result of the War of American Independence.

The British traders remain because they had set up a good trading system with the Indians which the Spanish could not duplicate. The U.S. didn't like the fact that the British were trading with the Seminoles. The Spaniards let the British continue trading with the Seminoles because the Indians distrusted the Spanish.

Cowkeeper vowed to kill 100 Spaniards, and at his death encouraged his successor to continue, because he was 14 short of his goal.

1788 - William Augustus Bowles proclaims himself Director General of the state of Muskogee and self-proclaimed leader of the Seminoles and Lower Creeks. Bowles was an English Tory from Maryland who became stranded in Pensacola as a teenager during the War of American Independence, and married into the local Creeks.

16 January 1792 - William Augustus Bowles with a large band of Creeks takes over and loots the Panton, Leslie, & Co. store in San Marcos (St. Marks).

1795 - The Treaty of San Ildefonso cedes all of West Florida above the 31st parallel to the United States.

31 October 1799 - William Augustus Bowles issues a proclamation declaring the 1795 treaty of San Ildefonso between Spain

& the U.S. void because it ignored the Indians' sovereign rights over Florida.

10 May 1800 - William Bowles is finally able to force the Spanish fort at San Marcos to surrender to him.

23 June 1800 - A large Spanish force sails up the St. Marks River and recaptures Fort San Marcos. Bowles escapes.

17 August 1800 - A well-armed force of 272 Spaniards and Mulattoes sets out from San Marcos to destroy William A. Bowles' stronghold and Seminole town on Lake Miccosukee. They ran into problems from the beginning, and returned to San Marcos two days later, haven gone only a few miles with no guide.

5 January 1802 - Bowles takes a large force of Seminoles, Negroes, and pirates, and lays siege to San Marcos. This time he is unsuccessful and the siege ends after 10 days. Bowles' failure to take the fort discredits him among his Indian supporters.

20 August 1802 - Neighboring Seminoles sign a peace treaty with the Spanish at San Marcos. Even Bowles' strongest supporter signs, Chief Kinache of Miccosukee Town.

24 May 1803 - At a conference of the Creek National Confederacy at the town of Tukabatchee, Bowles declares himself king of all the Indian nations present. The next day American Indian Agent Benjamin Hawkins had gained enough supporters to have Bowles captured and placed in irons, and delivered as prisoner to the Spanish governor in Pensacola. Bowles was taken to Morro Castle prison in Havana, where he died in 1805.

Part 3

1800-1815: Invasion & War in the Southeast

Fort Mims, Alabama, from Moore's <u>Indian Wars of the United States</u>.

1804 - Osceola is born near Tallassee, Alabama.

1807 - Coacoochee (Wildcat) is born on an island in Lake Tohopekaliga, Central Florida.

1810-1813 - The United States gains part of West Florida from the Mississippi River to the Perdido River, setting the present western boundary of Florida.

1811 - James McQueen dies at the age of 128. He was a Scotsman who joined the Tallassee Creeks and became an important leader among them. His son Peter McQueen took charge of the band after his father's death, and was great-grand-uncle of Osceola.

September & October 1811—Shawnee leader Tecumseh (his mother was Shawnee-Creek) travels to Creek country and talks to the Creek National Council at Tuckabatchee. Although he fails to unite the Creeks under his cause of a native movement against the United States, several Red Stick Warriors who support him return with Tecumseh up north.

17 March 1812 - American "Patriots" led by Colonel Thomas Smith occupy Fernandina and declare Florida as United States territory.

12 April 1812 - Colonel Smith's force occupies Fort Moosa near St. Augustine. They are forced to pull back after an attack by the Spanish & their free Black allies. Smith sets up an encampment further back from town. The Spanish burn Fort Moosa.

18 June 1812 - The War of 1812 begins as the United States declares war on Great Britain.

17 July 1812 - The Florida Indians finally have enough of the raids by the Americans in East Florida. The Spanish governor allows them to attack Georgia with the aid of former slaves. The Seminoles start by attacking illegally established American settlements on the St. Johns River.

9 September 1812 - Seminoles and their Black allies boldly attack and destroy the storehouses at the American outpost at Picolata on the St. Johns River, despite the presence of 250 Georgia Volunteer soldiers.

12 September 1812 - A supply train traveling between the American encampment at St. Augustine to Fort Stallings (on Davis Creek, Duval County) is attacked by a large number of Black Seminoles and Seminole Indians in the Twelvemile Swamp. Marine Captain Williams, commanding the supply train, is badly wounded and dies two weeks later.

24 September 1812 - Colonel Daniel Newnan with 117 Georgia Volunteers start a 3-week rampage through Florida. His objective is to attack King Payne and the Seminole town of Lotchaway at Alachua prairie.

27 September 1812 - Colonel Newnan's force runs into King Payne and about 75 Seminole warriors. A fierce battle lasts into the night with neither side getting the advantage. The Georgia force builds a breastwork for defense, but it also cages them in and cuts off any escape. King Payne, now over 80 years old, bravely leads the Seminoles, but is wounded and dies a few months later.

4 October 1812 - Facing starvation, Newnan's force decides to make a nighttime retreat from their breastwork.

5 October 1812 - Newnan's force continues to be attacked by Seminoles while making their retreat.

11 October 1812 - Newnan's force makes it back to Kingsley Plantation for a hero's welcome party. Their dismal failure was proclaimed a victory in the newspapers, and Newnan is declared a hero.

7 February 1813 - Colonel John Williams and Colonel Thomas Smith lead a force of Eastern Tennessee Volunteers into northeast Florida. They descend on Payne's Town at Alachua but find it deserted, having been abandoned weeks before. A few roving bands of harmless old men and women are found and shamelessly attacked by the Tennessee Volunteers.

10 February 1813 - The Williams & Smith Tennesseean force runs into a heavily defended Seminole position in a hammock near Payne's Town. There is no advance by either side and the battle lasts into the night. The Americans retreat to Paynes Town. Two days later they try to attack the Seminoles again, but are under sporadic fire from the Seminoles.

17 February 1813 - The Williams & Smith force leaves the Alachua area, with the final destruction of Paynes Town. Much of the Seminole's food supplies, crops, and cattle were destroyed by the campaign, and the Seminoles are faced with starvation.

24 February 1813 - The Tennessee force returns to Georgia as heroes. They parade around their only prisoners: one boy, one woman with a baby, one wounded woman, and one elderly Negro. They claim that only one of the Tennessee soldiers was killed. For over a year later, roving bands of Patriots loot and burn Indian villages and kill any Seminoles they find in northeast Florida.

10 April 1813 - An army report details an attack of Creeks under Little Warrior, who kill 7 whites at the Duck River in Tennessee. This is one of the incidents leading to the First Creek War. The Creek warriors were supporters of the Shawnee leader Tecumseh and his plan of uniting all the Tribes against the Americans. Later, the Creek National Council apprehends the attackers and has them executed.

22 July 1813 - Battle at Tuckabatchee. The Upper Creek Town of Tuckabatchee is surrounded by Red Stick Warriors, who attack the town that is friendly to the United States. Local American Mississippi territory militia soldiers come to help, but find the town abandoned. This is the beginning of the First Creek War.

27 July 1813 - Battle of Burnt Corn Creek in Southern Alabama. Territorial Mississippi Militia soldiers ambush Creek

Peter McQueen's supply train coming back from Pensacola with gunpowder. The Creeks are driven off, but they return and retake the supplies from the militia and chase them off. The militia soldiers who attacked McQueen's caravan were from Tensaw & Fort Mims northeast of Mobile.

30 August 1813 - Red Stick Creek Indians under Red Eagle (William Weatherford) attack Fort Mims and kill most of the occupants. Many of the Americans killed were actually mixed blood White and Creek settlers. Red Eagle was reluctant to lead, and only did when his fellow Red Sticks threatened him. He left in disgust when the non-combatants were killed against his wishes. Many of the Red Stick force were killed during the attack, and an estimated 250 of the settlers killed inside the fort. This caused the U.S. to turn its attention towards the Creeks.

1 September 1813 – The Kimbell-James Massacre in Clark County, Alabama. Josiah Francis is said to have led Red Stick warriors who attacked the Kimbell & James homesteads and killed 12 members of the James & Kimbell families.

2 September 1813 – The Battle at Fort Sinquefield, Alabama. While a burial service was being held for the Kimbell family members killed the day before, Red Stick Warriors attack the nearby fort. At first the warriors tried to catch the women washing by the spring, but 60 dogs released from the fort allowed the settlers to run inside the fort and defended the stockade for two hours until the Creeks disappeared.

3 November 1813 - A Tennessee Volunteer Militia force under Andrew Jackson, surrounds and attacks the Red Stick town of Tallushatchee. Over 200 people in the town are killed, included all the men. Any surviving women and children are taken prisoner. The quick and brutal attack was said to be in revenge for Fort Mims. David Crockett took part in the battle and said, "We shot them like dogs."

9 November 1813 - Jackson slaughters Red Stick forces at the Battle of Talladega, killing over 300 warriors. Lack of supplies forced him to abandon chase of the Creek survivors. Jackson is plagued with starvation and desertion of his troops until the next January.

12 November 1813 – The "Canoe Fight" battle in Alabama. A group of local militia sees a group of Red Stick Warriors on the Alabama River, and a running skirmish ensues. Captain Sam Dale with two other soldiers and a slave launch a canoe, and attack & defeat a canoe with 11 Red Stick warriors.

18 November 1813 - Tennessee soldiers & Cherokee allies under General James White attack and massacre the town of Hillabee. The town had already surrendered to Andrew Jackson, but poor communications between Tennessee forces made White's command unaware of the surrender. The Hillabee people felt that they were betrayed, and the survivors rejoin the Red Sticks for the remainder of the war.

29 November 1813 – The Georgia Militia under General Floyd attacks the Creek town of Autossee on the Tallapoosa River. Over 200 Red Sticks are killed including Creek Chief Hopoithle Micco. Floyd takes a musket ball to the knee.

23 December 1813 – Battle of Holy Ground in Alabama. Mississippi Territorial soldiers with a large number of allied Choctaw and Creek warriors under General Ferdinand Claiborne advance towards the Creek town of Econochaca, occupied by Red Stick forces under Weatherford and Josiah Francis. The soldiers are discovered before the battle, which give the town residents time to evacuate. The soldiers attack and burn the town. The next day the soldiers burn Weatherford and Sam Moniac's plantations, even though Moniac supported the Americans.

12 January 1814 - American Patriots establish Fort Mitchell in northeast Florida. They establish the "District of Elotchaway of the Republic of East Florida", and claim the land for the United States. (Today the area of Alachua and Marion Counties.) They have no support from the United States government or Georgia, and are forced to abandon Florida after their leader

Buckner Harris is killed by Indians on 5 May 1814. By that time, the Alachua Seminoles and free Black Seminoles have moved to Suwannee Old Town or Tampa Bay.

22 January 1814 – The Battle of Emuckfau Creek, Alabama. Andrew Jackson with 1000 troops on the way to attack the town of Tohopeka is himself attacked. Creek forces under Peter McQueen try three times to surround Jackson's encampment, but are fought off with artillery and cavalry charges.

24 January 1814 – The Battle of Enitachopco Creek, Alabama. Creeks again attack Jackson on his way back for supplies. Jackson's army are able to defend themselves again, but are forced to retreat back to Fort Strother.

27 January 1814 - The Battle of Calabee Creek. A large Red Stick Creek force under Paddy Walsh ambush Georgia forces at Camp Defiance in Alabama, with a high casualty rate on the Georgia side.

27 March 1814 – The Battle of Horseshoe Bend, Alabama. Andrew Jackson attacks the Red Stick town of Tohopeka and totally destroys it, ending the Creek War. Jackson's soldiers kill over 800 Creek warriors, and it is said that there were no more than 10 Red Stick warriors who survived. Women and children who tried to flee across the river are shot down by

Tennessee and Choctaw sharpshooters. Peter McQueen's band survived because he moved them away from Horseshoe Bend before the battle. It is believed that a young Osceola and his mother were captured in the area but released. McQueen and the Prophet Josiah Francis are also captured, but escape.

After March 1814 - Red Stick refugees move to Florida, making the Florida Indian population around 7,000. Osceola and his mother move into Florida around this time.

May 1814 - The British train and supply their Indian and free Negro allies, and established a fort for them on the Apalachicola River at Prospect Bluff, known as Negro Fort.

9 August 1814 - Andrew Jackson forces the Creeks to sign the Treaty of Fort Jackson, ceding 22 million acres of Creek land to the United States, including what is today most of Alabama and a large part of Georgia. Of the 36 chiefs who sign the treaty, only one was hostile to the United States in the previous war. Jackson felt that his allies also needed to cede their land because they could have prevented the Creek War by stopping the hostiles. Jackson does not give any option to the Creeks except sign.

After Jackson defeated the Creeks, one of the largest and most powerful Native American nations east of the Mississippi, the whites were convinced that no Indians could stand against them and the westward expansion.

15 September 1814 – British forces fail to capture Fort Bowyer at Mobile Bay from the Americans. The British land force includes 180 Seminole or Miccosukee Indians from Florida. The British had failed to take the fort because John Innerarity of John Forbes & Co. had warned the Americans in advance. The retreating British and their Indian allies loot the Forbes store at Bon Secour in retaliation.

7 November 1814 - Andrew Jackson takes Pensacola from the Spanish with almost no effort. He leaves two days later for New Orleans. The British store arms and gunpowder in Fort Barrancas, but blow it up when they evacuate before Jackson arrives.

14 December 1814 to 9 January 1815 - An American force under Major Uriah Blue rampages through West Florida, destroying several Indians towns, and killing or capturing any Indian found.

23 December 1814 to 8 January 1815 - The Battle of New Orleans. Several hundred Miccosukee and Seminole Indians side with the British at the Battle of New Orleans, including Chief Bowlegs. They are not at the actual battle, but waiting to be deployed from ships anchored miles away.

11 February 1815 – American forces surrender Fort Bowyer at Mobile Point to the British after several days of siege, rather than have the fort destroyed and all inside killed. Two days later, word reached the area that the war is over.

Part 4

1816-1818: The First Seminole War

"The Scott Massacre." Major Muhlenberg's boat going to Fort Scott is ambushed in November 1817. From Moore's Indian Wars of the United States.

27 July 1816 – An American supply ship on the Apalachicola River comes under fire from Negro Fort, a fortification of escaped slaves and Indians that was built and supplied by the British at the end of the War of 1812. A red-hot cannon shot from the American ship hits the fort's powder magazine and immediately destroys the fort in a huge explosion. The American's Creek Indian allies loot the remains. Most all the

300 people who were inside the fort are killed instantly by the explosion.

21 November 1817 - The First Seminole War starts as General Edmund P. Gaines attacks Fowltown, a Seminole town on the Flint River in Georgia just north of the Florida border. Town Chief Neamathla had prevented any Americans from traveling the Apalachicola River to Fort Scott or to approach Fowltown.

30 November 1817 – "The Scott Massacre." A Creek/Seminole force under Neamathla retaliates for the destruction of Fowltown, and attacks an American boat under Major Muhlenberg traveling up the Apalachicola River, killing 34 soldiers, 7 women, and 4 children. Six soldiers escape to Fort Scott.

26 December 1817 - The Secretary of War authorizes Andrew Jackson to take command of the situation along the border between Florida and Georgia and bring the Seminoles under control.

4 January 1818 - Americans from Fort Scott go to attack Fowltown, but find it deserted and burn it to the ground instead.

9 March 1818 - Jackson arrives at Fort Scott and assembles a force of 2,000, including Creek Indians friendly to the United States, regular Army soldiers, and Tennessee volunteers. He heads south and burns and loots any Seminole and Free Black village that he finds in north Florida.

14 March 1818 - Jackson's force reaches the former Negro Fort and establishes Fort Gadsden as a supply base.

20 March 1818 - Warriors under Savannah Jack ambush Soldiers near Fort Claiborne, Alabama. Several are killed, including Captain William Butler, whom the local county is named after.

29 March 1818 - Jackson's force destroys the Seminole/Miccosukee village of Tallehassa near Lake Miccosukee.

1 April 1818 - Jackson attacks Miccosukee, the huge village complex of Chief Kenhaggee on Lake Miccosukee. The town is abandoned by the time Jackson arrives. They find many scalps believed to be taken from local settlers in Florida and Georgia over the past few years. The town's food stores are burned. Many of the Florida Indians face starvation after Jackson's rampage.

6 April 1818 - Jackson forces the Spanish at Fort San Marcos (St. Marks) to surrender. British Indian trader Alexander Arbuthnot is captured.

7 April 1818 - An American ship anchored off St. Marks and flying a British flag captures Red Stick leaders Himathlemico and Josiah Francis. They are hanged the next day. Jackson leaves St. Marks and heads towards Suwannee Old Town.

12 April 1818 - Battle of Econfina River. Creek allies of Jackson under William

MacIntosh attack Peter McQueen's village. 37 of warriors are killed; the highest casualty rate of a single battle during the First Seminole War. 14-year-old Billy Powell (Osceola) and his mother are taken prisoner but released by promising to bring in Peter McQueen. Osceola and his mother eventually move to the town of Talakchopco along Peas Creek (Peace River). McQueen is never captured and dies a couple years later at Cape Florida.

16 April 1818 - Jackson reaches Suwannee Old Town, a large Seminole town under the leadership of Chief Boleck (Also known as the first Chief Bowlegs.) The town was already warned of Jackson's advance and had previously evacuated. Black Seminoles put up a strong defensive action to allow more time for the women and children to escape to the other side of the river. British Marine Officer Robert Ambrister is captured.

29 April 1818 - Jackson orders a trial and quick execution of the British prisoners Alexander Arbuthnot and Robert Ambrister. They were charged with inciting the Indians to wage war against the United States. Although there was little evidence and Arbrister is recommended for punishment & release, Jackson orders the executions. General Gaines as President of the Court sentences Arbuthnot to be hung and Ambrister shot. This causes outrage in

Britain, and Jackson has to defend this action for years to come.

28 May 1818 - Jackson forces the surrender of Fort Barrancas and Pensacola and then leaves for his home in Tennessee. Congress is outraged by his actions of invading Spanish territory and hanging British citizens.

16 September 1818 - Soldiers pursue and battle warriors under Savannah Jack over a large area in Butler County of southern Alabama.

Part 5

1819-1834: Treaties Written, Treaties Broken

Chief Neamathla from the McKenny-Hall paintings by the Dept. of Interior.

1819 - Spain realizes that she can not keep control of Florida and cedes it to the United States with the Adams-Onis Treaty. This was not a purchase; the United States agrees to pay the claims of American citizens against Spain for up to five million dollars from the last ten years of border disputes. There is no evidence that any claims were ever paid. The treaty also sets the border between the US Louisiana Purchase territory, and Texas & Mexico.

22 February 1821 - The Senate ratifies The Adams-Onis Treaty, and it is signed by President James Monroe, making Florida US territory. Congress appoints Andrew Jackson as the first Governor of Florida Territory.

Prominent Florida citizen Moshe Levy with Edward Wanton establish a settlement and trading post for the Indians near the modern town of Micanopy, and Chief Micanope becomes the head leader of the Seminoles. The Indians persuade the friendly white traders to go to St. Augustine and inquire about the Indian's status with the United States. Jackson arrives as governor and removes the white traders as negotiators for the Indians, saying that only congress can appoint an Indian agent.

17 April 1822 - William DuVal becomes territorial governor.

29 July 1822 - Governor DuVal issues a proclamation against whites doing unethical trade against the Indians or settling near Indian towns, but is powerless to enforce it.

1823 - A government census estimates that there are 4883 Indians in Florida. (Actual number is probably greater.)

18 September 1823 - Governor DuVal negotiates the Treaty of Moultrie Creek with the Florida Indians. Neamathla is picked to lead the Seminole delegation. The minutes of the treaty negotiations are incomplete, with whole days unrecorded. It is not known what happened at the actual negotiations and how the treaty articles came about.

The Indians agree to stay in central Florida under provisions of the treaty. The government agrees to protect them as long as they obey the law, and agrees to provide livestock, food, and annuity payments of $5000 for 20 years. The government also agrees to keep unauthorized whites off the reservation and maintain an agent on the reservation. The Indians agree not to encourage former slaves to fight against the U.S. There is no provision on how long the treaty was to be in effect; later the Seminoles claim that it had to be at least 20 years, because that is how long the annuity payments were to be paid. Unfortunately the government totally fails to provide the food provisions, with either no food or rancid beef.

The Indian Agency under Gad Humphreys moves to a location near what is today the present city of Ocala in 1825. Fort King is established near the agency in 1827. Fort Brooke at Tampa Bay is established in 1824.

Under the treaty, Neamathla is given a small area of land to settle in the Apalachicola Valley along with a few other chiefs who were friendly towards the United States. Neamathla later loses it because of his hostility towards the United

States and dissatisfaction over failure of the government to carry out provisions in the treaty. In 1826 he moves to Alabama. In 1836 at the age of 84, he participates in the Second Creek War in Georgia and Alabama as one of the most successful war chiefs.

Governor Duval, Commissioner James Gadsden, and Secretary of War John Calhoun in correspondence suggest that the Seminoles should be sent west of the Mississippi.

Abraham, Black Seminole leader. Served as translator and aide to Micanopy. From Sprague's The Florida War.

23 December 1823 - The U.S. Senate ratifies the Treaty of Moultrie Creek.

The U.S. Supreme Court declares that all land in America is owned by the right of discovery and conquest, and that the aboriginal inhabitants have no right or claim on the land. This basically invalidates the Treaty of Moultrie Creek because the Supreme Court declared that Indians didn't have any rights to the land.

26 July 1824 - Governor DuVal removes Neamathla as head chief of the Seminoles and replaces him with Tuckose Emathla (John Hicks).

30 April 1825 - Creek Indians surround the house of Coweta Chief William MacIntosh and execute him for illegally signing the Treaty of Indian Springs which sells the remaining Creek lands over to the United States.

May 1826 - Seminole leaders including Neamathla, Tuckose Emathla, and Abraham visit Washington to plead their case to remain in Florida. The Americans try to impress upon the Seminole leaders the military strength of the Americans.

December 1826 - Captain Francis L. Dade responds to Indian attacks in Georgia and northern Florida by leading an expedition up the Suwannee River. Dade destroys many Seminole villages and forces the residents into the confines of the Seminole Reservation. By April 1827 Dade had scouted out and cleared Creek and Seminole Indians from the Aucilla River to

Suwannee River, and along the Gulf Coast. Dade shows brutal efficiency for chasing after Indians.

28 May 1830 - The Indian Removal Act is narrowly passed in congress and signed by President Jackson. All tribes east of the Mississippi River are to be removed to the west.

24 March 1832—The Treat of Cusseta cedes all Creek land east of the Mississippi to the United States. The Creeks were given the option of receiving an allotment of land for individual families, but the practice ignored the difference in the matriarchal culture where the females are the land owners. The Creeks were subjected to the worst example of land fraud in the history of the United States where titles for land were fraudulently sold or traded until the Creeks were dispossessed from their land and forced into removal.

9 May 1832 - The Treaty of Payne's Landing with the Seminoles is signed. No minutes were taken of the negotiations, so it is not known what happened at the talks. Later, many of the chiefs denied that they had signed.

The treaty said that the chiefs would inspect the western lands and decide if it was good enough for them to emigrate, and that they would reunite with the Creeks. Rumor is that Abraham was bribed to misinterpret the talks in order to get the chiefs to sign. The chiefs said that the Seminoles were not obligated to follow them to the west, and that they had only agreed that they would inspect the land.

Osceola making his mark on the treaty. Although a popular story, there is no historical documentation to confirm the incident. The story first appeared in poetry a couple years after Osceola's death.

10 October 1832 - Several of the Seminole chiefs are taken on a tour out west to survey the land that the government had reserved for them. The group includes Jumper, Tuckose Emathla (John Hicks), Holata Emathla, Charley Emathla, Abraham, Coa Hadjo, Yaha Hadjo, and Neha-Thlocco.

28 March 1833 - The Treaty of Fort Gibson is signed. The treaty states that the Seminoles would move out west within three years. Later the chiefs either denied that they had signed the treaty, or that they had signed it only with the understanding that they would survey the land. Charges were that the Indians had been made drunk and coerced into signing the treaty, or that Seminole Indian Agent John Phagan had forced them to sign. Phagan was later removed from office on charges of malfeasance, fraud, and improper conduct. The treaty was later declared invalid, but was enforced by President Jackson anyway.

1 December 1833 - Wiley Thompson arrives from Georgia as the new Indian Agent at Fort King. He was picked by Jackson because it was believed that he could quickly remove the Seminoles from Florida.

8 April 1834 - The U.S. Senate approves the treaties of Payne's Landing and Fort Gibson after President Jackson waits several months to submit them to the senate for a vote.

24 April 1834 - John Eaton replaces DuVal as territorial governor of Florida. Eaton, as the former Secretary of War, left Washington over the "Petticoat Affair" scandal that resulted in nearly all of President Jackson's cabinet resigning. Two years later when the Second Seminole War had started, Eaton was replaced by Richard K. Call and become ambassador to Spain.

23-25 October 1834 - Wiley Thompson calls the Seminole chiefs together for a conference at Fort King to get them to emigrate, but it ends with both sides arguing and no agreement reached.

24 November 1834 - General Duncan L. Clinch becomes the overall military commander of the Florida forces.

General Duncan L. Clinch.

Part 6

1835: Crisis as War Begins Again

Dade's Battle, from Moore's <u>Indian Wars of the United States</u>, 1858. Of the various illustrations done of the battle in the 19th Century, this one is fairly accurate.

13 January 1835 - Assassination attempt against President Andrew Jackson by unemployed painter Richard Lawrence at the U.S. Capitol building in Washington. Lawrence was judged insane because he claimed that he was King of Britain and America, and that Jackson had conspired with the British at the Battle of New Orleans to take his throne and fortune.

16 February 1835 - President Jackson orders all Seminoles to leave Florida.

27 March 1835 - Indian Agent Wiley Thompson and General Duncan Clinch have another unsuccessful conference with the Seminole chiefs to try and persuade them to emigrate west.

23 April 1835 - A third conference is conducted at Fort King where Thompson tries to convince the Seminole chiefs to emigrate to the west. Thompson declares that all the chiefs not present and don't agree to emigrate are no longer leaders of their people, including Micanope and Arpeika (Sam Jones). Even President Jackson disagrees with Thompson's actions, saying that it is up to the Seminoles to decide who will be their leaders.

May 1835 - Thompson puts Osceola in irons for disorderly conduct until he agrees to bring in his people and emigrate to the west.

19 June 1835 – Seminoles and local settlers fight over cattle and reservation boundaries at Hickory Sink, south of what is today Gainesville. A small party of Indians engaged in butchering cattle are discovered by local militia soldiers who overpower and start whipping them. Two other Indians arrive and a gunfight ensues. One Indians is killed and another wounded.

11 August 1835 - Miccosukees kill the mail carrier between Fort Brooke and Fort King. It is believed that this was in response to the Hickory Sink incident.

10 November 1835 - Several brigades of the Florida Militia are mustered in service to force removal of all Florida Indians.

14 November 1835 - Five chiefs with 450 Seminoles arrive at Fort Brooke to emigrate west.

26 November 1835 - Assassination of Chief Charlie Emathla. General Thompson holds a sale for Indians to sell their cattle before emigrating west. After selling his cattle, Charlie Emathla is executed by Osceola, who scatters the money on the ground next to the body. It is said that the body remained untouched on the ground for years as Osceola's warning to all Seminoles who wanted to emigrate. A previous Seminole council had declared a sentence of death on anyone who sold their cattle to the white man.

30 November 1835 - General Thompson warns white inhabitants of Florida to expect increased Indian attacks.

November or December 1835 - Skirmish in Alabama near Hobdy's Bridge in Pike County between 75 Creeks and 150 Militia soldiers.

1 December 1835 - General Thompson sets another sale for Indians to sell their livestock before moving west. This time, no one participates.

7 December 1835 - The Florida militia fights Seminoles in a hammock near

Wacahoota, at the plantation of Captain Gabriel Priest.

On the same day, Seminoles attack a woodcutting party on Drayton's Island, at Lake George on the St. Johns River.

17 December 1835 - Seminoles attack plantations near Micanopy.

18 December 1835 - The "prelude" battle of the Second Seminole War, later known as the Battle of Black Point. Seminoles believed to be under Osceola attack a Florida Militia supply train near Wacahoota on a road going from Newnansville to Micanopy in Alachua County. Many of the militia soldiers deserted the battle at the first sign of attack, leaving only a few that are unable to defend the wagons against a larger force. Eight soldiers are killed and six or eight wounded.

20 December 1835 - Florida Militia forces attack a Seminole camp and recapture their wagons from the battle two days earlier. The militia get back their papers and cooking utensils, but not their ammunition and clothing.

25-27 December 1835 - Seminoles attack and destroy the Cruger, Depeyster, Stamp, Hunter, and Dunham plantations south of St. Augustine. Over the next few weeks, King Philip, his son Coacoochee, and Creek & Yuchi Indians under Yuchie (or Uchee) Billy, lead a campaign that destroys all the plantations and settlements on the East Coast south of St. Augustine.

Bulow Plantation ruins. Photo by the author

26 December 1835 - Seminoles overrun and destroy the Dunlawton plantation (New Smyrna.)

On the same day, Seminoles destroy the Hillsboro lighthouse near present day Fort Lauderdale.

26-27 December 1835 - The sugar plantation owned by Major Benjamin Heriot are attacked and burned by King Philip's band, who captures 75 slaves.

28 December 1835 - Dade's Battle. Major Francis L. Dade's command is ambushed on the military road between Fort Brooke and Fort King. Only three of the 110-man command survives. The Seminole force is estimated around 180 warriors with only a few casualties. This is the Seminole's most significant victory in the war.

At the same time, Indian agent Wiley Thompson and Lieutenant Constantine Smith are ambushed and killed outside Fort King by warriors under Osceola. The sutler store is also attacked and burned.

29 December 1835 - The Rees Plantation is destroyed at Spring Garden.

31 December 1835 - First Battle along the Withlacoochee River. About 250 Seminoles under Alligator and Osceola fight 250 regular army troops under General Duncan Clinch, as 460 Florida Volunteers watch on the opposite bank. Osceola is injured during the battle. After the battle, the Americans retreat back to Fort Drane.

Part 7

1836: Seminoles Claim the First Victories and Another Creek Uprising

General Winfield Scott from an 1850's biography.

1 January 1836 - Deadline set by Indian Agent Wiley Thompson for the Seminoles to emigrate west by the Treaty of Paynes Landing and Fort Gibson. Thompson was killed four days earlier.

6 January 1836 – "New River Massacre" in southeast Florida. Indians kill members of the Cooley family and burn their homestead near present day Fort Lauderdale.

9 January 1836 - Skirmish near Micanopy.

12 January 1836 - 200 mounted Florida Volunteer Militia soldiers under Colonel Parish have "a sharp encounter with a large body of Indians near Wetumpka," believed to be in present-day northwest Marion County. They are ambushed by Seminoles but are able to drive them off. As night fell, the militia stayed in a defensive position at the battlefield until leaving the next morning.

13 January 1836 - General Hernandez abandons Bulowville plantation because there are not enough soldiers to defend it from attack. The Seminoles burn the structures shortly after.

17 January 1836 - Florida Militia soldiers fight Seminoles near Old Town while crossing the Suwannee River.

18 January 1836 - Major Benjamin Putnam's "Mosquito Roarers" Florida Militia unit retreats from the Dunlawton plantation after an attack by King Philip & Coacoochee's force.

21 January 1836 - President Jackson orders General Winfield Scott to take command of the forces in Florida.

26 January 1836 - General Winfield Scott arrives in Florida and soon comes in conflict with General Edmund Gaines over the military operations. Gaines had been ordered to proceed to the Texas frontier, but instead took a force of 500 regulars and 700 Louisiana Volunteers to Tampa Bay to fight the Seminoles. Gaines' western department included west Florida, but Scott had been given command of the Florida forces. Scott later blames Gaines for ruining his surprise campaign against the Seminoles, and Gaines blames Scott for intentionally abandoning him to the Indians without support on the Withlacoochee River.

26 January 1836 - Bryants Ferry on the Chattahoochee River, in Stewart County, Georgia. A company of local militia fires upon a group of 40 peaceful Chehaw Creeks camping along the river. When the Creeks come to retrieve the bodies of their people under a white flag, Georgia troops fire on them again. A skirmish ensues and the Creeks chase the Georgians back to Columbus.

20 February 1836 – Eight weeks after Dade's battle, General Gaines' command is the first white group to reach Major Dade's command and buries the bodies.

27-29 February 1836 - The Seminoles attack the General Gaines' command at the Withlacoochee River. The soldiers are forced to retreat down the river and make a hastily built breastwork (Camp Izard) for defense. Gaines' command lay under siege for the next week.

General Edmund P. Gaines

6 March 1836 - The siege on the Withlacoochee ends when General Gaines negotiates an end with Alligator, Jumper, Osceola, and Abraham. Soldiers arriving from Fort Drane during the negotiations mistakenly fire upon the Indians and chase them away.

10 March 1836 - South Carolina militia soldiers battle at the Addison Blockhouse on the Tomoka River. Three soldiers are killed. The Indians were probably Miccosukees of King Philip's band.

13 or 14 March 1836 - Skirmish between Florida Militia and Indians between Tampa and Alafia River.

16 March 1836 - The U.S. Senate confirms Richard K. Call as the territorial governor of Florida to replace John Eaton. Eaton steps down the following month.

March-April 1836 - General Scott starts a three-pronged campaign to attack the Seminoles in the Cove of the Withlacoochee. The campaign ends in failure, with the three armies never meeting up with each other.

General Eustis' command crossing the Oklawaha River in March 1836.

22 March 1836 - A command under General Abraham Eustis is attacked while crossing the St. Johns River at Volusia.

25-26 March 1836 - The Seminoles harass an army command under Colonel Lindsay during an attempt to cross the

Withlacoochee River. The Seminoles are driven off when a canon is fired at them.

26 March 1836 - A large Seminole force attacks a Florida Militia force searching the hammocks near Fort Brooke (Tampa). The militia drives off the Seminoles with the loss of one soldier killed and one wounded.

28 March 1836 - Skirmish at Fort Broadnax, near "Chickuchatty."

29 March 1836 - General Eustis' command is attacked while they are bivouacked on the Oklawaha River.

29-30 March 1836 - Seminoles battle General Scott's command at the Camp Izard crossing on the Withlacoochee River. A running skirmish continues the next day.

30 March 1836 - General Eustis' army and Seminoles skirmish near the Seminole village of Okihumpky. The village is burned, but Eustis gives up plans to pursue the Seminoles in the cove of the Withlacoochee. The Seminoles now have almost total control of the interior of Florida.

5-17 April 1836 - A Georgia Volunteer Battalion establishes Fort Cooper to observe the Cove of the Withlacoochee. They are under heavy siege until reinforcements arrive about two weeks later.

12-15 April 1836 - After guarding a blockhouse on the Withlacoochee River for six weeks, an army company under Captain Holleman is attacked by a large force of Seminoles. A force from Fort Brook rescues the soldiers after a messenger is sent. The company guarding the blockhouse had been forgotten by General Scott.

20 April 1836 - The Seminoles make a night attack on Fort Drane.

27 April 1836 - The Seminoles attack an army garrison dismantling Fort Alabama (later reactivated as Fort Foster) at nearby Thlonotosassa Creek. The soldiers booby trap the powder magazine and hear a large explosion after they leave.

Reconstructed Fort Foster at Hillsborough River State Park north of Tampa. Phot by the author.

5 May 1836 - The 2nd Creek War begins. Neamathla and Jim Henry are seen as the main leaders as Creek warriors attack white settlements along the Chattahoochee River, and between Columbus, Georgia, and Tuskegee, Alabama. Col. William Flournoy is shot dead a few miles from Fort Mitchell, Alabama.

8 May 1836 - Skirmish near General Hernandez's plantation. (Today Palm Coast in Flagler County, Fla.)

13 May – Creek warriors attack a stagecoach near Fort Mitchell, Ala.

15 May 1836 - Young Hitchiti Creek leader Jim Henry leads a Creek Indian force that destroys the town of Roanoke, Georgia. The survivors flee to Columbus. Steamboats along the Chattahoochee River are attacked.

The same day, soldiers with the Alabama militia from Chambers County destroy Loachapoka Town, although most of the residents had already fled.

15 & 16 May 1836 – Creek warriors ambush several more stagecoaches near Frazier's Stand & Brush Creek. Traffic ceases along the federal road between Montgomery, Alabama, and Columbus, Georgia, stopping all communication and business between the cities.

19 May 1836 - Quartermaster General of the Army Thomas Sidney Jesup becomes commander of the western troops involved in the Creek war, but soon comes in conflict with General Scott over conflicting tactics and strategies. The Jackson administration starts to implement removal of the Creeks even though they had not signed a final removal treaty.

3 June 1836 – Eufaula Creeks attack settlers in Pike County, Alabama.

Georgia troops fire upon Creeks crossing the Chattahoochee River at Watson's plantation south of Columbus.

4 June 1836 – The steamboat *Metamora*, is fired upon by a large number of Creek warriors from the shore about 20 miles south of Columbus, Georgia. Georgia and Alabama militia troops hiding on board fire back and drive away the Creeks.

9 June 1836 - Soldiers under siege at Fort Defiance (near the town of Micanopy) use bold and unorthodox battle maneuvers to drive away Seminoles under Osceola.

9 June 1836 - Battle of Shepherd's Plantation in Stewart County, Georgia. Creeks lure Georgia militia forces under Captain Garmany into an ambush and almost surround them. The Georgians retreat and are pursued by Creek warriors for three miles with several of the militia killed.

16 June 1836 – Georgia troops in southwest Georgia sight Indians, which causes them to panic and flee to Fort Jones.

18 June 1836 - General Jesup comes to destroy Neamathla's fortified village on Hutchechubbee Creek in Alabama. Due to the slow movements of the troops, the town residents had already fled. Neamathla had been captured a few days before.

22 June to 22 October 1836 - A company of Florida Militia from Columbia County have several battles against the

Creeks in the Okefenokee Swamp area, claiming to have killed and taken prisoner many Indians.

25 June 1836 - The Secretary of War appoints Florida Governor Richard K. Call as commander of the forces in Florida.

25 June 1836 – Creek warriors moving down to Florida kill up to 15 settlers near Chickasawhatchee Creek. It is believed that these killings were in revenge for the settlers taking Creek land.

1 July 1836 – Creek leader Jim Henry surrenders. General Scott declares the Creek War in Georgia and Alabama over. The announcement is premature. 84 year old Neamathla and hundreds of his warriors are marched 90 miles in chains from Fort Mitchell to Montgomery, Alabama. Scott's report estimates that there are only about 200 Creeks still at large in the swamps or on their way to Florida.

2 July 1836 - The Battle of Chickasawhachee Swamp in Baker County, Georgia. Georgia Militia soldiers rout the Indians from an almost impenetrable island in the swamp and secure all the Indian's supplies and food.

7 July 1836 – Alabama militia soldiers find Creek warriors in Cowikee Swamp and give chase, but are driven out by the Creeks.

8 July 1836 – General Winfield Scott leaves Columbus Georgia, ordered to Washington D.C. by President Jackson. Scott declares the war over and thinks that the Georgia militia would just do small mop-up operations, but he was wrong.

10 July 1839 – skirmish on the Alapaha River in Georgia.

15 July 1836 - Battle of Brushy Creek. The Georgia militia pursues and attacks Creeks retreating into Florida. At the beginning of the battle, the Indians have the advantage, but with the arrival of more troops, they are forced to retreat and disappear into the swamp. The Creeks left in such a hurry that babies were found abandoned and dead.

19 July 1836 - Battle of Welika Pond near Micanopy. 250 Seminoles under Osceola ambush 52 troops guarding a supply wagon, but the troops defend themselves until reinforcements arrive.

23 July 1836 - Spanish Indians attack and burn the Cape Florida lighthouse.

24 July 1836 – Skirmish at Quarles Plantation near Wesley Chapel in Stewart County, Georgia near Lumpkin. The Georgia militia chases after Creeks, but are nearly surrounded, panic, and chased off by the Creeks in a scenario that is often repeated during the Creek War in Georgia.

25 July 1836 – Stewart County (Georgia) Rangers head towards the Chickasawhatchee Swamp to fight with the Creeks, and soon find them at Jones Plantation south of Lumpkin. The undisciplined soldiers are easily beaten and retreat.

27 July 1836 – Skirmish at Ichawaynotchaway Creek in Baker County, Georgia. Stewart County Rangers attack a Creek encampment in a hammock from two different sides, and have a bloody and difficult battle until completely driving away the Creeks.

27 July 1836 - Battle on Travers plantation on the St. Johns River. The army surprises a group of Seminoles but has to retreat when they are out-gunned.

28 July 1836 - Skirmish at the mouth of Black Creek at Ridgely's Mill. A group of soldiers bringing horses from St. Augustine to Garey's Ferry are attacked by a large number of Indians.

5 August 1836 – Major Julius Alford of the Georgia Militia has a bloody battle with Creek Warriors east of Chickasawhatchee. Although there are no confirmed kills, bloody evidence remained. In the two week campaign in Georgia, the only confirmed kill of a Creek was an old man who was shot and killed by two boys when he got near a settler's cabin.

13 August 1836 – The battle of Brushy Creek in south Georgia. Georgia militia troops trying to drive Creeks out of the area find warriors entrenched in a fortified position. After a skirmish, the Georgia troops are driven off and many of them just desert and run home. Another Georgia battalion arrives and is also driven away. After the battle, the Georgians retrieve 35 Creek prisoners from a local jail who had been turned in by local settlers, and show them off as prisoners of war from their "victorious" campaign.

21 August 1836 - 300 Miccosukees under Osceola who have taken over the abandoned Fort Drane battle 100 army troops. After an hour the Indians disappear into the nearby hammocks.

Late August 1836 – Skirmish near Pindertown south into Irwin County, Georgia. Desperate fight between the Georgia Militia and the Creeks, where even the Creek women are fighting hand-to-hand.

27 August 1836 - Battle of Cow Creek in southern Georgia. Georgia militia forces find and attack Creeks who are heading into the Okefenokee Swamp.

1 September 1836 - 759 Creeks are recruited by the United States Army to become Indian scouts and mediators against the Seminoles in Florida.

18 September 1836 - The Battle at San Felasco Hammock. 100 Florida volunteers and regular army troops drive back a large Seminole force.

30 September 1836 - Skirmish near Tampa Bay.

8 October 1836 - Seminoles capture and burn the schooner *Mary* at Tavernier Key.

13-17 October 1836 - Governor Richard K. Call starts his campaign against the Seminole as commanding general of forces in Florida, by trying to cross the Withlacoochee River and attack the Seminoles. His efforts end in failure with no adequate crossing and constant fire by Seminoles from the other side.

17-18 November 1836 – Fighting in the area of Wahoo Swamp. Forces under General Call find scattered groups of Seminole but only have a few small skirmishes.

21 November 1836 - Battle of Wahoo Swamp. Forces under General Call have a large battle with heavily encamped Seminole and Black Seminole forces, but are unable to dislodge their position on the opposite side of a creek. Major David Moniac of the U.S. Creek Regiment is killed. Moniac was the first Indian to attend West Point Military Academy.

30 November 1836 - Thomas Lawson becomes Surgeon General. He was an officer with the Louisiana Volunteers under General Gaines at Fort Brooke during the beginning of the 2nd Seminole War.

9 December 1836 - General Thomas Sidney Jesup replaces General Call as the commander of the forces in Florida.

December 1836 - The Marine Commandant, Colonel Archibald Henderson, leaves Washington, D.C. and joins the fighting in Florida. A few months earlier he had participated in the Creek War.

Part 8

1837: Betrayal and Defeat

An 1851 illustration of Osceola. From the author's collection.

17 January 1837 - A Militia force from St. Augustine engages Black Seminoles at Hanson's plantation. John Caesar, a very important Black Seminole leader, is killed in the battle.

23 January 1837 - Army forces attack an Indian camp near Lake Apopka. Chief Osuchee (known as Cooper) is killed, and is the most important chief killed thus far in the war.

26 January 1837 – Creek warriors attack the Pugh plantation in Barbour County, Alabama and kill Mr. Pugh and some slaves. When the local militia arrives the next day, they find Indians still there, open fire, but the soldiers are driven off.

27 January 1837 - The Battle of Hatchee-Lustee Creek (Reedy Creek near Lake Tohopekaliga.) Large battle where Army and Marine forces find and overrun a large Indian camp. The army captures dozens of horses with pack saddles, and the Indians are left without supplies.

28 January 1837 – Alabama Militia soldiers pursing Creek warriors who raided the Pugh plantation have a heavy fight at Martin's Creek and Cowikee Creek.

3 February 1837 - Jumper, Micanope, and Abraham agree to a cease-fire until 18 February, but it soon becomes obvious that not all the Seminoles agree to it.

3 February 1837 - Skirmish between Alabama Militia and Creek Indians near Cowikee Creek, southeast Alabama.

5 February 1837 – Georgia militia soldiers come into Alabama and drive peaceful Creeks from their camp near Tuskegee who were awaiting removal. The soldiers then loot Creek livestock, money, and belongings left behind. The disgruntled Creeks who were awaiting removal join the resistance instead, and the fighting begins anew.

8 February 1837 - Battle of Lake Monroe. 300-400 Miccosukee/Seminoles attack Camp Monroe under the leadership of Coacoochee and King Philip, with Louis Pacheco, a survivor of Major Dade's command. Captain Mellon is killed during the battle, but the soldiers are able to repel the attack with firing from a howitzer on a steam ship. The camp is renamed Fort Mellon after the fallen Captain.

9 February 1837 - Colonel Foster finds and destroys an encampment of Seminoles on Crystal River, but the Indians escape.

10 February 1837 - Skirmish with Creek Indians and Alabama Militia along Pea River in Alabama at Hobdy Bridge. The militia over runs the Creek's position, and the Creeks scatter and run, leaving behind their provisions.

19 February 1837 – Alabama militia raid a camp of friendly Creeks at Pole Cat Springs, Alabama. They loot and rape the innocent Creek families. These were the families who had their men away in Florida fighting as the Creek regiment on the side of the United States.

5-6 March 1837 - General Jesup starts negotiations at Fort Dade to have the

Seminoles immediately cease hostilities and emigrate to the west. Seminole leaders Jumper, Cloud, Abraham, Alligator, and Coacoochee participate in the negotiations.

General Thomas S. Jesup

20 March 1837 – Alabama troops have a skirmish with Creek warriors raiding the Ellison plantation in southern Alabama.

24 March 1837 - Battle along the Pea River in Alabama near Hobdy Bridge; probably the bloodiest battle of the 2nd Creek War. Alabama Militia forces find an Indian camp in the swamp. At first the soldiers are chased off, but another column is able to cross the river and enter the camp. Many of the soldiers are firing in the water at a heavily defended position. The battle lasts for almost four hours with heavy casualties on both sides. There is close hand-to-hand combat with even Creek women from the camp fighting and firing weapons. The soldiers eventually take the camp with a cost of about a dozen casualties, and about 50 Creeks killed.

29 March 1837 – A letter published in a Florida newspaper from Andrew Jackson insults the Florida Volunteer Militia Soldiers. Jackson says that he could take 50 women and beat the Seminoles, and that Florida women should let their men die so they can remarry and have children who won't grow up to be cowards. Jackson just finished his two terms as president, and Martin Van Buren is now the new President.

10 April 1837 - Deadline set by the Fort Dade agreement for the Seminoles to be ready at Fort Brooke to emigrate west. Because of a slow turnout, Jesup allows the deadline to be extended.

15 April 1837 – When a Creek family goes to Lumberton (Florida) on the Blackwater River to trade for supplies, settlers brutally killed one warrior and imprison his wife and child. This incident helped spark the Creek uprising in west Florida.

23 April 1837 – Creek warriors attack a cow camp on Gum Creek and kill five cattlemen in response for the Lumberton incident the week before. This starts murders and raids in northwest Florida and southern Alabama. The Hart family in Dale County, Alabama is killed, and the local militia track the raiders and kills 14 of them in Florida.

19 May 1837 – Walton County militiamen fight the Creeks at Battle Bay near Cow Ford on the Choctawhatchee River. Several Creeks are captured.

23 May 1837 – Florida militia troops track down and capture Creeks camped on Alaqua Creek (Walton County) and a nearby homestead. The militiamen slaughter their captive prisoners, scalp them, and then cut silver jewelry off their bodies in one of the worst massacres during the war. There was never any formal investigation into the incident.

2 June 1837 - Osceola, Sam Jones (Abiaka), and Coacoochee appear at the Seminole encampment near Fort Brooke during the night. By daybreak all the Seminoles (over 700) who have been waiting to emigrate, disappear into the Florida swamps with supplies of food and ammunition. Other causes for the mass exodus may have been due to a measles outbreak, or threats by white slave traders in the area. General Jesup submits his resignation as commander of Florida forces, but is rejected.

25 June 1837 – A wood cutting party of five civilians lands on Key Largo and is ambushed by Indians. Ship Captain John Whalton and one sailor are killed.

Coacoochee or Wild Cat. From John T. Sprage's Florida War.

4 July 1837 – Florida militiamen raid a large Creek encampment with a battle on the Shoal River (Okaloosa County) and capture the belongings and packs of the Indians. Among the items captured is the gold watch of William Flournoy, who was killed by Euchee warriors in 1836.

19 July 1837 – Florida militiamen find a Creek town in the Alaqua Swamp and pursue the Creeks and battle at the Creek encampment, but most of the Creeks escape.

9 September 1837 - Army troops surprise and overrun a Seminole encampment near the Tomoka River. King Philip is captured.

10 September 1837 - Battle of Mosquito Inlet. Army troops surround and capture Yuchie (or Uchee) Billy and his camp. 2nd Lt. John Winfield Scott McNeil is killed, nephew of future President Franklin Pierce.

18 September 1837 - The last of the U.S. Army Creek Indian Scouts are released from service in Florida. Many are ill and dissatisfied with the treatment they received. Their families are sent west after waiting for removal at Fort Morgan, Alabama.

21 October 1837 - A large Seminole party under Osceola is captured under a flag of truce at Fort Peyton by General Hernandez, under orders of General Jesup.

25 November 1837 - Yuchie Billy dies at Fort Marion in St. Augustine.

29 November 1837 - Coacoochee, John Cowaya (an influential Black Seminole leader, also know as John Cavalo, Gopher John, or John Horse) and 18 others make a daring night escape from their prison at Fort Marion in St. Augustine.

December 1837 – The number of armed American forces in Florida numbers around

9,000 soldiers, sailors, marines, and state militia forces, which includes 56% of the total regular U.S. Army.

The Battle of Okeechobee, from Moore's Indian Wars of the United States. As was common for the time, it is not a very accurate depiction of the battle.

25 December 1837 - Battle at Lake Okeechobee. Colonel Zachary Taylor leads a command of soldiers against a combined Seminole and Miccosukee force less than half their number. Seminole leaders who participate are Sam Jones, Coacoochee, Alligator, Otolke-Thloco, and Halleck Tustenuggee. Taylor routs the Indians from a hammock on the north side of Lake Okeechobee, but sustains the second largest number of soldiers killed and highest number wounded of any battle during the war. The 6th Infantry and the Missouri

Militia suffer the most casualties. Still, the battle is declared a victory and heightens Taylor's military and future political career.

26 December 1837 - General Nelson's Georgia Volunteers battle a wandering band of Seminoles on the Wacasassa River.

Part 9

1838: Retreat to the Everglades

Reconstructed Fort Christmas east of Orlando. Photo by the author.

1 January 1838 - Seminole prisoners at St. Augustine are moved to Fort Moultrie, South Carolina. Included are Micanope, Coa-Hadjo, Little Cloud, King Philip, Osceola, and 200 others.

15 January 1838 - A small naval expedition under Lt. L.M. Powell falls under heavy attack by Seminoles on the Loxahatchee River near Jupiter Inlet.

24 January 1838 - The Battle of Loxahatchee/Jupiter Inlet. Heavy fighting in a well-defended hammock along the Loxahatchee River. General Jesup is wounded in the face during the battle. For numbers involved, this is the largest battle during the war.

31 January 1838 - Osceola dies and is buried at Fort Moultrie, South Carolina. His physician Dr. Weedon secretly removes Osceola's head before burial for his private medical specimen collection.

2 February 1838 - Skirmish in the Everglades.

3 March 1838 - Seminole prisoners at Fort Moultrie, South Carolina are moved to Indian Territory in the west. King Philip dies during the journey.

22 March 1838 - Battle of Pine Island in south Florida. A large party of army and militia find and overtake Seminole camps on Pine Island. Although not many Seminoles are killed or captured, the surprise attack makes them lose their entire supplies.

24 April 1838 - Battle at Sam Jones' camp in the Everglades.

29 April 1838 - Indians attack an Army escort near Micanopy and kill three soldiers, two of which were recruits.

15 May 1838 - Zachary Taylor, recently promoted to Brigadier General, replaces General Jesup as commander of the forces in Florida.

20 May 1838 - Seminoles kill several soldiers near Fort Clinch on the Withlacoochee River.

27 May 1838 - Skirmish in Okefenokee Swamp on the Florida / Georgia border between the Florida Militia & Seminoles.

4 June 1838 - Seminoles burn the abandoned Fort Dade and the bridge on the Withlacoochee River. The Seminoles disappear after a short skirmish.

17 June 1838 – "Battle of Kanapaha Prairie." Army forces find and attack a Seminole camp in a hammock at Kanapaha Prairie. Captain Walker of the local militia who is acting as guide is killed, leaving the soldiers lost in the woods for several hours.

18 June 1838 - Skirmish along the Ochlocknee River.

26 July 1838 – Creek warriors raid a homestead on the Ocklockonee River, killing the settlers, raiding food, and kill all the livestock they are unable to take with them.

16 August 1838 - "Fort Norton" skirmish, on the East Side of the Okefenokee Swamp northwest of Colerain, Georgia. Seminoles attack a wagon train.

August 1838 - A company of Army Dragoons attempts to explore the Okefenokee Swamp in Georgia searching for renegade Creeks and Seminoles. The expedition ends in utter failure without a single Indian found.

28 October 1838 - The remaining bands of the Seminoles who lived along the Apalachicola river on land given to them in the 1823 Treaty of Moultrie Creek are deported to the west.

27 December 1838 - Skirmish near the Econfina River.

General Zachary Taylor

Part 10

1839-1840: The Bloody War of Attrition

Secretary of War Joel Poinsett

1839 - 2nd Seminole War veteran John Harris becomes Commandant of the Marine Corps.

11 February 1839 - Skirmish near New River Inlet, southeast Florida.

20 February 1839 - Skirmish near Fort Lauderdale.

28 February 1839 - Skirmish on the Miami River.

20 March 1839 - Indians attack a surveying party at Itonia Scrub in northeast Florida.

2 May 1839 - Skirmish near Fort Frank Brooke; two soldiers killed.

18 May 1839 - The Commanding General of the Army, Major General Macomb, visits Florida and declares the war over after negotiations with two Miccosukee leaders. Two weeks later, Seminoles camped around Fort Brooke disappear, and attacks by anti-removal bands continue.

Commanding General of the Army Alexander Macomb

20 May 1839 - Skirmish "between Forts No. 3 and No. 4."

12 June 1839 - Army patrol attacked by Indians near Fort Cross.

21 July 1839 - Skirmish "between Forts Frank Brooke and Andrews."

23 July 1839 – Seminoles/Spanish Indians under Chakaika & Hospetarke attack and burn a trading post on the Caloosahatchee River manned by 2nd Dragoon Regiment soldiers. Many soldiers are killed. Colonel William S. Harney escapes. General Macomb's cease fire agreement with the Seminoles is now considered voided.

29 August 1839 - Battle near Fort Andrews; two soldiers killed.

10 September 1839 - Indians attack a military escort near Fort Fanning.

27 September 1839 - Skirmish near Fort Lauderdale.

9 November 1839 - Skirmish between the Florida Militia and Seminoles in the area of Micanopy. At least one soldier killed and two wounded.

25 November 1839 - Skirmish in the area between St. Augustine and Picolata.

29 November 1839 - Secretary of War Joel Poinsett, disappointed with the long duration of the war, writes President Van Buren to remove Governor Call. Robert Reid becomes governor soon after.

21 January 1840 - Skirmish "near Suwannee."

24 January 1840 - Skirmish at Fort New Smyrna.

The same day there is listed a skirmish "near Fort Preston" in the Florida panhandle.

1 February 1840 - Skirmish "near Fort No. 5." An Army patrol is ambushed while crossing a causeway.

4 February 1840 - Seminoles capture a supply train of 12 wagons, 10 miles from Gary's Ferry.

9 February 1840 - The Florida Militia engages Seminoles in a skirmish at Fort Crabbe.

10 February 1840 - Skirmish "near Fort No. 3."

13 February 1840 - A mail stage is held up and two carriers killed north of St. Augustine.

22 February 1840 - Skirmish near Magnolia where the officer, Lt. Whedan, is left by his men that run off when ambushed by Seminoles.

March 1840 – A change of presidents causes Governor Reid to be replaced by former Governor Call.

10 March 1840 - Methodist minister McRea is killed by Indians and buried at Martin's Point between Micanopy and Wacahoota.

18 March 1840 - Seminoles attack an empty supply train between Fort No. 2 (Fort Hook) and Micanopy.

24 March 1840 - Seminoles attack a party of soldiers with cattle near Fort King. Two soldiers are also killed at the fort within 200 yards of the pickets.

10 April 1840 - An expedition of Marines and Navy sailors lands on Cape Sable and are attacked by a large force of Seminoles. The naval force defends itself for a few hours until rescued, without loss of any man.

The same day there is a skirmish near Fort Wool.

12 April 1840 - Skirmish between Forts Griffin and Fanning.

14 April 1840 - One soldier killed on patrol near Fort King.

21 April 1840 - General Taylor receives permission to leave Florida after he requests to be relieved of command. Colonel Twiggs of the 2nd Dragoon Regiment becomes acting commander of the forces in Florida until a general officer can replace Taylor.

23 April 1840 - Massacre at the McLane homestead in Gadsden/Liberty County area.

24 April 1840 - Skirmish near Fort Lauderdale.

25 April 1840 - Indians attack a supply train near Fort Barker; one soldier killed.

28 April 1840 - Battle near Fort King. Captain Gabriel Rains sets explosive traps outside of Fort King in retaliation for recent attacks against his soldiers. While checking a device that had exploded the night before, a large body of 120 Indians in a hammock attacks the company of soldiers numbering 17. The Indians are said to be Miccosukees under the leadership of Halleck Tustenuggee. The soldiers are almost surrounded but fight their way out in a desperate battle. Rains is severely wounded along with several of his men. Four Indians are killed. Captain Rains lives on to become known as the father of land mines.

5 May 1840 - Brigadier General Walker Armistead takes over the command of the army in Florida from Colonel David E. Twiggs.

19 May 1840 - The Battle of Bridgewater. An Army courier is attacked between Forts Wacahoota and Micanopy. A 7th Infantry command of about 18 soldiers from Fort Micanopy searching for the attackers are ambushed by a large number of Seminoles. (Probably Miccosukees under Halleck Tustenuggee.) 11 soldiers are killed and four missing, making this one of the deadliest skirmishes in the war.

23 May 1840 - Seminoles under Coacoochee attack a company of actors at Picolata Landing on the St. Johns River and steal their costumes. They then surround nearby Fort Searle to try and force the soldiers out to fight, but the badly outnumbered soldiers stay inside.

24 May 1840 - The Florida Territorial papers state that Fort Crum (Alachua County) is wiped out by Indians with all but one settler killed. The source is third-hand information, so it is doubted, or the writer may have confused it with the Battle of Bridgewater. No other sources confirm this event.

12 July 1840 - Skirmish at Cow Creek Hammock.

13 July 1840 - Skirmish near Fort Pleasant; two soldiers killed.

16 July 1840 - Indians attack Fort Russell.

26 July 1840 - Skirmish near New River Inlet.

29 July 1840 - Skirmish on the Wekiva River in central Florida. Soldiers locate and overrun Coacoochee's camp.

7 August 1840 - Chakaika and the Spanish Indians attack and burn the town of Indian Key. This is the only battle during the war where the Indians find and use an artillery piece.

13 August 1840 - Indians attack an Army escort and kill two soldiers near Fort Wheelock.

30 August 1840 - Seminoles attack an army escort near Micanopy. Two soldiers are killed, and another is captured and tortured to death.

6 September 1840 - Seminoles attack near Fort Wacahoota; two soldiers killed.

1 November 1840 - Skirmish on the Picolata Road; three soldiers killed.

William S. Harney from Reavis, <u>The Life and Military Services of William Selby Harney</u>, 1879.

3-24 December 1840 - Forces under Colonel William S. Harney leave Fort Dallas (Miami) searching for Seminole villages in the Everglades. The army forces wear Seminole clothing and travel in dugout canoes, in a Special Forces type of operation. This is the first time Americans cross Florida through the Everglades.

9 December 1840 - Col. Harney's force discovers and destroys a Seminole village in the Everglades. Six women and children are captured. Soldiers pursued and captured two warriors who are immediately hung.

10 December 1840 - Col. Harney's force finds Chekika's Island hideout, and discovers that he is the one who burned the trading post and attacked his command on the Caloosahatchee the previous year. Chekika is killed and hanged with his captured warriors, and the women and children are taken prisoner to Fort Dallas.

28 December 1840 - Miccosukees under Halleck Tustenuggee & Coosa Tustenuggee attack an Army escort on the Micanopy-Wacahoota road and kill six people, including Mrs. Montgomery, the wife of Lt. Alexander Montgomery (7th Infantry) at Fort Micanopy. The death of Mrs. Montgomery causes outrage in newspapers across the country, and Secretary of War Joel Poinsett demands an investigation.

Historic interpreters at Dade Battlefield, January 2010; photo by author. Steve Abolt (far right) portrays a commanding officer of the US Seventh Infantry Regiment at events all over the country. The US 7th suffered greatly in Florida in 1840 with many battle casualties.

Part 11

1841: Unending Campaign Against the Seminoles

FIGHTING IN FLORIDA.

"A Dragoon soldier fighting in Florida." In reality, it was not as glamorous as this illustration portrays. The 2d Dragoon Regiment had more deaths than any other regiment in Florida, and many in combat. From Reavis, <u>The Life and Military Services of William Selby Harney</u>.

January 1841 - Seminoles attack Fort Walker in Alachua county and kill several people.

22 January 1841 - Battle near Fort Lauderdale.

2 March 1841 - Battle at the crossing between Fort Brooke on the Oklawaha River and Fort Russell on Orange Creek. Heavy fighting. Indians are believed to be Miccosukees under Halleck Tustenuggee.

3 March 1841 - Skirmish near Fort MacKay (Ocala Forest) involving the same Indians as the day before. The Indian camp is found on March 5th, with items recovered include the coat of Lt. Sherwood and cloak of Mrs. Montgomery who were killed at Martin's Point the previous December 28th.

5 March 1841 - Coacoochee comes to Fort Cummings for peace talks. He is dressed as Hamlet, and other chiefs are wearing Shakespearean costumes raided from the troupe of actors the previous year.

1 May 1841 - Lieutenant William T. Sherman escorts Coacoochee to Fort Pierce.

May 1841 – The entire Florida Militia is discharged from duty because of the high war costs. Only regular army troops are used in Florida after this point.

31 May 1841 - General Armistead is relieved of command because of Washington's political turmoil and the fact that the war has not ended yet.

After 25 June 1841 - Major General Winfield Scott becomes Commanding General of the U.S. Army after the death of Alexander Macomb. He holds this post until 1861.

4 July 1841 - Coacoochee is held as prisoner to convince other Seminoles to surrender.

16 July 1841 - Skirmish at an Indian camp on the Oklawaha River. One soldier is killed while charging alone into the camp.

17 July 1841 - Skirmish near Camp Ogden.

31 August 1841 - Colonel William J. Worth becomes commander of the forces in Florida.

2 September 1841 - Three citizens are killed at Martin's Point between Micanopy and Wacahoota.

25 September 1841 - Skirmish near Fort Russell. Indians attack an Army escort with supply wagons camped for the night.

12 October 1841 - Coacoochee with 210 Seminoles are shipped to the west.

October 1841 - John C. Spencer becomes Secretary of War after Secretary Bell resigns.

25 October 1841 - Several soldiers drown when their boat capsizes at the Indian River crossing. This is the worst non-combat related accident during the war.

20 December 1841 – Miccosukee Indians under Halleck Tustenuggee attack Mandarin Settlement on the St. Johns River south of Jacksonville.

The same day, Major Belknap fights a well defended group of Seminoles in Big Cypress

Swamp at "Prophet's Town." Two soldiers are killed and buried in the swamp. The Indians disappear without any captured.

Part 12

1842: The End of the War

William J. Worth

25 January 1842 - An Infantry detachment attacks Halleck Tustenuggee's camp at Haw Creek near Dunn's Lake (Crescent Lake), but the Indians escape.

12 February 1842 - Skirmish in the Wahoo Swamp.

19 April 1842 - Colonel Worth leads an attack on Halleck Tustenuggee's camp at Peliklakaha Hammock near Lake Ahapopka

(Apopka.) Army forces take the camp and defending position, but the Indians escape. One soldier killed in the battle is buried in the muck of the surrounding swamp. This is the last battle of the Second Seminole War.

10 May 1842 - Secretary of War Spencer notifies General Scott that the administration wants the war to end soon at discretion of the commander in Florida.

17 May 1842 - Two soldiers killed on patrol near Fort Wacahoota.

Also the same day, Indians shoot at an Army patrol on the Suwannee River. One soldier receives fatal wounds and dies at Fort Fanning. These are the last soldiers killed by Indians during the war.

13 June 1842 - David Levy, U.S. Delegate in the House of Representatives for the Territory of Florida, said no sympathy should be given to the Indians of Florida since they are not the aboriginal inhabitants of Florida, and had only moved there recently. (Even though the Seminoles were in Florida before the Americans.) It is believed that he made this speech in congress to keep the war going, with government money and military support coming into Florida.

14 August 1842 - Colonel Worth declares hostilities in Florida at an end, thus ending the Second Seminole War. He agrees to let the remaining Seminoles stay in south

Florida. After this time there are still a few isolated reports of attacks by Seminoles, and a few more Indians are shipped west.

15 August 1842 - A memorial ceremony is held at St. Francis military cemetery in St. Augustine in honor of all the soldiers who died in service in Florida during the war. Soldiers of all the regiments in the regular army are represented, and wagonloads of bones are buried under a three-pyramid monument.

Part 13

1842-1855: An Uneasy Truce

Fort Brooke barracks in Tampa; early 1900's postcard.

31 August 1842 – A large party of Creek warriors kill the Perkins family in Orange Hill, Washington County, Florida.

28 November 1842 - A Florida Militia company finds an Indian village on Wrights Creek (Holmes County) and kills 22 Indians, taking no prisoners. Even the local white settlers considered this a unprovoked massacre.

9 January 1843 - A band of Creeks under Chief Pascoffer surrenders at St. Marks and is sent out west.

17 November 1843 - General Worth estimates the Florida Indian population around 300.

8 January 1844 - A ship stops for repairs on Phillips Inlet (Bay County) and the crew is befriended by Chief Old Joe and his band. Later, Chief Joe kills several of the crew when they are lured inland away from the ship.

1845 - A census of the Indian population in Florida is estimated around 360.

3 March 1845 - Florida becomes the 27th State of the United States of America.

12 July 1849 - Four renegade Indians attack a settlement north of Fort Pierce.

17 July 1849 - Four renegade Indians, believed to be the ones who attacked the settlement near Fort Pierce the week before, attack the trading post on Paynes Creek, killing two clerks. This starts the "Panic of 1849" when several forts in Florida are reactivated with a threat of another war. It is never known if the renegades acted alone as outlaws, or were part of an aborted Indian uprising.

18 September 1849 – General David Twiggs meets with Billy Bowlegs, who turns over four of the renegades who had burned the settlement and trading post in July, ending the crisis and panic.

12 January 1852 - Aaron Jernigan, a settler near Fort Gatlin (Orlando), leads a posse of local settlers on a hunt for Seminoles. They find a village at Lake Tohopekaliga and kill some of the Seminoles, their livestock, and drive off 120 hogs. Several of the local citizens complain to the Governor Thomas Brown, but the governor defends Jernigan. Brown says that the Seminoles should not have been that far north of the reservation boundary, and that if the Indians had livestock, it must have been stolen.

20 September 1852 - After meeting with President Fillmore in Washington, Billy Bowlegs signs a treaty with three other Florida Seminole delegates whom agree to emigrate west. The Indians change their mind after harsh treatment from the whites and hearing about living conditions from their relatives out west.

12 January 1853 - A law is passed in Florida that makes it unlawful for any Indian to be within the borders of the state. Another law the same month makes it illegal to trade with the Indians.

Part 14

1855-1858: The Third Seminole War

Billy Bowlegs, from Reavis, <u>The Life and Military Services of William Selby Harney</u>.

18 December 1855 - Army surveyors in the Everglades find the camp of Billy Bowlegs and destroy his garden. When Bowlegs goes to the surveyors to complain, he is laughed off. (This story is not verified, but is generally believed to be true.)

20 December 1855 - Seminoles under Billy Bowlegs attack the camp of Army surveyors. Lt. George Hartsuff, the officer in charge, is seriously wounded. This is the beginning of the Third Seminole War.

18 January 1856 - Seminoles attack a wood cutting party from Fort Denaud on the Caloosahatchee River.

1 March 1856 - The number of federal and state troops in Florida numbers 1460 against an estimated 100 Seminole warriors.

2 March 1856 - Seminoles attack the Snell house on Sarasota Bayou.

29 March 1856 - Skirmish "near Chocoliska." (Chokoloskee Island?)

31 March 1856 - Seminoles attack the Braden plantation along the lower Manatee River.

3 April 1856 - Army troops attack the town of Oscen Tustenuggee at Charley Apopka Creek east of the Peace River. Two Indian scalps are taken by the army troops and displayed in local towns.

12 April 1856 - Seminoles burn and loot abandoned houses on the lower Manatee River. Three days later, the same Indians kill settler John Carney.

18 April 1856 - Army troops attack Billy Bowlegs' town. The Indians put up a good defense and escape.

2 May 1856 - Several companies of regular Army and Florida militia troops scout the Everglades in pursuit of Indians and burn abandoned villages.

14 May 1856 - Seminoles attack the Bradley house near Darby in Pasco County and kill Mrs. Bradley and two children.

17 May 1856 - A supply train going between Forts Brooke and Fraser is attacked with only one survivor.

11 June 1856 - Secretary of War Jefferson Davis writes a letter to Florida Governor Broome critical of the behavior and non-commitment of the Florida militia.

14-16 June 1856 - The Battle of Tillis Farm near Fort Meade. Fight between a large force of Indians against the Tillis family and local militia. The battle continued the next two days along the Peace River. Many important white and Seminole leaders are killed, including Oscen Tustenuggee. The white and Indian accounts of the battle vary widely, with no real victory by either side. This is the largest battle during the Third Seminole War because of the forces involved and the high casualty rate.

2 August 1856 - Seminoles kill a soldier guarding a blockhouse at Punta Rassa.

7 August 1856 - A delegation of Oklahoma Seminoles sign a treaty in Washington where the government will supply payments to the western Seminoles. This recognizes the Seminoles as separate from the Creeks for the first time.

September 1856 - Brigadier General William S. Harney becomes the commander of the forces in Florida.

17 December 1856 - Seminoles attack and burn a house near New Smyrna and kill the occupants. The Seminoles then burn several houses at Dunlawton. White settlers in northern Florida are panicked.

5 January 1857 - The army starts a vigorous pursuit against the Seminoles after several months of failed negotiations.

March 1857 - With a new presidential administration in Washington, John B. Floyd replaces Jefferson Davis as Secretary of War.

4 March - 23 April 1857 - Campaign to capture Indians in the Big Cypress Swamp.

April 1857 - General Harney is ordered to Fort Leavenworth, Kansas, and is replaced by Colonel Gustavus Loomis.

May 1857 - Seminoles attack an army detachment at Palm Hammock near Pavilion Key. Later the same month, they capture an army ammunition supply.

26 July 1857 - An army boat company captures a Seminole camp on the Kissimmee River near Lake Okeechobee.

15 August 1857 – Florida volunteers under Capt. Mickler capture many

Seminole women and children near the Kissimmee River.

26 August 1857 – Skirmish near Lake Istokpogo where the Florida mounted volunteers under Captain W.H. Kendrick destroy a Seminole village.

19 November 1857 - Army soldiers find and burn several Miccosukee towns in Big Cypress.

21 November 1857 – Skirmish west of Okaloocoochee Slough and south of Fort Doane where Florida mounted volunteers under Captain Cone capture a large number of Seminoles with supplies.

26 November 1857 - Indians retaliate for the attack on their towns and kill several army horses.

27 November 1857 - A force under Colonel S. St. George Rogers destroy a large Seminole village found at Royal Palm Hammock in the Big Cypress Swamp.

28 November 1857 – Captain John Parkhill of Leon County is killed in a skirmish near Royal Palm Hammock. (Believed to be in Fakahatchee Strand Preserve.) He is buried on the shore of what is probably Deep Lake in Big Cypress. In 1861, a monument is erected in his honor on the front lawn of the old capitol building in Tallahassee. Parkhill was the highest ranking officer killed during the 3rd Seminole War.

3 December 1857 – Last known skirmish of the 3rd Seminole War with Capt. Winston Stevens, Fla. Mounted Volunteers. A force of 91 regular Army infantry and Florida militia finds a large Seminole town, but are ambushed by a force of Seminoles and forced to retreat. This is believed to have taken place in the northern area of Big Cypress National Preserve.

1857 - Coacoochee dies of smallpox in Mexico. He had received a colonel's commission in the Mexican Army for defense of the Mexican frontier.

4 May 1858 - After two and a half months of negotiations, a large group of Seminoles under Billy Bowlegs and Assinwah emigrate to the west. The negotiation team is made up of Western Seminole John Jumper, Yucabatche Micco (a Creek), and Halleck Tustenuggee. The ship Grey Cloud carrying them stops at Egmont Key in Tampa Bay and picks up another waiting group of Indians. There are a total of 165 Indians who agree to emigrate. When the ship stops at St. Marks, a small party of Seminoles with Polly Parker go ashore to collect herbs and escapes.

8 May 1858 - Colonel Gustavus Loomis declares the Third Seminole War officially over, ending the last Indian war east of the Mississippi. The Indian population in Florida is estimated from 100 to 300.

Seminole bands remaining in Florida are under the leadership of Sam Jones, Chipco, and Ismahtree. Sam Jones is too old to lead the Seminoles or Miccosukees, so Chipco becomes the principal chief until about 1880.

February 1859 - 70 Seminoles from Black Warrior's band emigrate west. This is the last large group of Seminoles & Miccosukees that are shipped west.

1902 - Florida Governor William S. Jennings finally gets the U.S. Government to pay the salary of the state militia for the Third Seminole War.

1950 - The Peridido Band of Friendly Creek Indians of Alabama and Northwest Florida are organized. Calvin McGhee is the first Chairman. Today it is the Poarch Creek Tribe, and gained official recognition from the federal government in 1984.

1957 - The Seminole Tribe of Florida, Inc., is formed. Bill Osceola is the first Tribal Chairman.

1962 - The U.S. Government grants recognition to the Miccosukee Tribe of Florida, but they did not receive federal reservation land until the Indian Land Claims Settlement Act of 1982. Buffalo Tiger served as the first Chairman until 1986.

Billy Bowlegs III and family from an early 1900's postcard.

Bibliography:

Adjutant General's Office, Department of the Army
1964 (microfilm) "Letters Received," and "Reports to Congress" 1822-1860. Letters to the Secretary of War, organized as received at the War Department, United States National Archives and Records Service.

Andrews, Evangeline Walker, and Andrews, Charles McLean
1985, Jonathan Dickinson's Journal or, God's Protecting Providence. Being the

Narrative of a Journey from Port Royal in Jamaica to Philadelphia between August 23, 1696 and April 1, 1697., Florida Classics Library, Port Salerno, Florida.

Andrews, Mark
"Early Orange County Settler Finds Himself in Trouble with the Law", The Orlando Sentinel, Sunday, September 11, 1994.

Army and Navy Chronicle; weekly newsletter printed from January 1835 to May 1842, Washington.

Avant, David A., Jr.
1985, Illustrated Index, J. Randall Stanley's History of Gadsden County, L'Avant Studios, Tallahassee, Florida.

Bacon, Eve
1975, Orlando, A Centennial History, The Mickler House Publishers, Chuluota, Florida.

Bemrose, John
1966, Reminiscences of the Second Seminole War, edited by John K. Mahon, University of Florida Press, Gainesville.

Best, Christine Kinlaw
2003, The History of Fort Mellon, Sanford, Florida, Including: Fort Reid, Fort Lane, Fort Kingsbury, The Second Seminole War 1836-1842, The Sanford Historical Society, Inc., Sanford, Florida.

Blackman, William Fremont
1973, <u>History of Orange County Florida</u>, The Mickler House Publishers, Chuluota, Florida.

Blakey, Arch Fredric
1976, <u>Parade of Memories, A History of Clay County, Florida</u>, Clay County Bicentennial Steering Committee.

Board of County Commissioners, Suwannee County
1958, <u>Suwannee County Centennial, September 28 to October 4, 1958</u>, Souvenir Program.

Boone, Floyd E.
1988, <u>Florida Historical Markers & Sites</u>, Gulf Publishing Company, Houston, Texas.

Bowles, William Augustus
1791, <u>Authentic Memoirs of William Augustus Bowles</u>, Arno Press & The New York Times. 1971 Reprint Edition.

Boyd, Mark F.
<u>Florida Aflame, The Background and Onset of the Seminole War, 1835</u>, reprint from The Florida Historical Quarterly, XXX, (July 1951) 3-115.

Brady, Tom
1998, <u>2nd Seminole War Letters of Fort Micanopy</u>, Micanopy, Florida.

Braund, Kathryn E. Holland
2012, <u>Tohopeka; Rethinking the Creek War & the War of 1812,</u> The University of Alabama Press.

Brown, Jr., Canter
　1991, <u>Florida's Peace River Frontier</u>, University of Central Florida Press, Orlando, Florida.
　The Florida Crisis of 1826-1827 and the Second Seminole War, Florida Historical Quarterly, LXXIII, (Apr. 1995) 419-455.

Brown, George M., Ord. Sergt., U.S.A.
<u>Ponce de Leon Land and Florida War Record</u>, 7th edition, 1902, The Record Co., St. Augustine, Florida.

Brown, Tom O.
Locating Seminole Indian War Forts, Florida Historical Quarterly, XL, 310-313.

Bullen, Adelaide K.
1965, <u>Florida Indians of Past and Present</u>, University of Florida, Gainesville.

Bullen, Ripley P., and Griffin, John W.
An Archaeological Survey of Amelia Island, Florida, The Florida Anthropologist, Vol. V, nos. 3-4, (December 1952) 37-64.

Bunker, George E.
1975, <u>Swamp Sailors</u>, University Press of Florida, Gainesville.

Bunn, Mike, and Williams, Clay
2012 (Second printing), <u>Battle for the Southern Frontier; the Creek War and the War of 1812</u>, The History Press, Charleston, S.C.

Campbell, Richard L.
1892, <u>Historical Sketches of Colonial Florida</u>, part of the Floridiana Facsimile Series, University Press of Florida, Gainesville, 1975.

Carswell, E.W.
   1986, <u>Holmsteading, The History of Holmes County, Florida</u>, Rose Printing Company, Tallahassee.
   1991, <u>Washington, Florida's Twelfth County</u>, Rose Printing Company, Tallahassee.

Carter, Clarence E.
1956-1962, <u>Territorial Papers of the United States, Vols. XXII-XXVI: Florida Territory</u>. Washington.

Clark, Agnew Hilsman
<u>History of Stewart County Georgia, Volume II, with Family Histories Edited Annotated and Indexed by Agnew Hilsman Clark and Marean Moncrief Clark</u>, Waycross, Georgia.

Cobb, Samuel E.

The Spring Grove Guards, Florida Historical Quarterly, XXII, (Jul. 1944), 208-216.

Coe, Charles H.
   1898, <u>Red Patriots: The Story of the Seminoles</u>, part of the Floridiana Facsimile Series, University Press of Florida, Gainesville, 1974.
   The Parentage and Birthplace of Osceola, Florida Historical Quarterly, XVII, (Apr. 1939), 304-311.

Cohen, Myer M.
1836, <u>Notices of Florida and the Campaigns</u>, part of the Floridiana Facsimile Series, University of Florida Press, Gainesville, 1964.

Coker, Edward C., and Schafer, Daniel L.
A West Point Graduate in the Second Seminole War: William Warren Chapman and the View From Fort Foster, Florida Historical Quarterly, LXVII, (Apr. 1990), 447-475.

Coker, William S.
   1981, <u>The Last Battle of the War of 1812: New Orleans. No, Fort Bowyer! (Now Fort Morgan at Mobile Point.)</u>, The Perdido Bay Press, Pensacola.
   The Papers and History of Panton, Leslie and Company, and John Forbes and Company, Florida Historical Quarterly, LXXIII, (Jan. 1995), 353-358.

Covey, Cyclone
1990, <u>Cabeza de Vaca's Adventures in the Unknown Interior of America</u>, 5th printing, University of New Mexico Press, Albuquerque.

Covington, James W.
   The Establishment of Fort Brooke, Florida Historical Quarterly, XXXI, (Apr. 1953) 273-278.
   The Indian Scare of 1849, Tequesta, # XXI, 1961, 53-64.
   The Florida Seminoles in 1847, Tequesta, # XXIV, 1964, 49-58.
   "The Yamassee Indians in Florida: 1715-1763", The Florida Anthropologist, Vol. 23, no. 3, (September 1970) 119-128.
   1982, <u>The Billy Bowlegs War, 1855-1858, The Final Stand of the Seminoles Against the Whites</u>, The Mickler House Publishers, Chuluota, Florida.
   Billy Bowlegs, Sam Jones, and the Crisis of 1849, Florida Historical Quarterly, LXVIII, (Jan. 1990) 299-311.
   1993, <u>The Seminoles of Florida</u>, University Press of Florida, Gainesville.

Craig, Alan K., and Peebles, Christopher S. Captain Young's Sketch Map, 1818, Florida Historical Quarterly, XLVIII, (Oct. 1969), 176-179.

Cubberly, Frederick

Fort King, Florida Historical Quarterly, V, (Jan. 1927) 139-152.

Davis, T. Frederick
   The Seminole Council, October 23-25, 1834; and, Letter of Colonel James Gadsden on the Seminole Council, Florida Historical Quarterly, VII, (Apr. 1929) 330-356.
   "United States Troops in Spanish East Florida, 1812-1813"; Part I, Florida Historical Quarterly, IX, (Jul. 1930), 3-23. Part II, IX, (Oct. 1930), 96-116. Part III, IX, (Jan. 1931), 135-155. Part IV, IX, (Apr. 1931), 259-278. Part V, IX, (Jul. 1931), 24-34.

Denham, James M.
"Some Prefer the Seminoles": Violence and Disorder Among Soldiers and Settlers in the Second Seminole War, 1835-1842, Florida Historical Quarterly, LXX, (Jul. 1991), 38-54.

Dibble, Ernest F.
Captain Hugh Young and His 1818 Topographical Memoir to Andrew Jackson, Florida Historical Quarterly, (Jan. 19), 321-346.

Dodd, Dorothy
Jacob Houseman of Indian Key, Tequesta, VIII, (1948) 3-19.

Drake, Samuel G.

1880, Aboriginal Races of North America, 15th edition, Hurst, New York.

DuBois, Bessie Wilson
1981, The History of the Loxahatchee River, Southeastern Printing Co., Stuart, Florida.

Dysart, Jane E.
Another Road to Disappearance: Assimilation of Creek Indians in Pensacola, Florida, During the Nineteenth Century, Florida Historical Quarterly, LXI, (Jul. 1982), 37-48.

Ellis, Gary D.; and GARI
1999, The Nature Coast and Its Cultural Environment, Volume III: Notes on the Seminole Wars, Gulf Archaeology Research Institute, Crystal River, Florida.

Ellison, John T.
2010, The Second Creek War; Interethnic Conflict and Collusion on a Collapsing Frontier, The University of Nebraska Press.

Ervin, William R.
1983, The Seminole War, Prelude to Victory, 1823 - 1838, W.&S. Ervin Publishing Co., Holly Hill, Florida.

Eyster, Irving R., and Brown, Darlene
1976, Indian Key, Jeannie's Magic Printing, Long Key, Florida.

Fishburne, Jr., Charles C.

1982, <u>Of Chiefs and Generals, A History of the Cedar Keys to the End of the Second Seminole War</u>, Sea Hawk Publication, Inc., Cedar Key, Florida.

Flanigan, James C.
1943, <u>History of Gwinnett County, Georgia, Volume I</u>, Tyler & Company, Hapeville, Georgia.

Florida Department of Military Affairs
   <u>Special Archives Publication Number 72</u>, State Arsenal, St. Francis Barracks, St. Augustine, Florida.
   <u>Special Archives Publication Number 149</u>, State Arsenal, St. Francis Barracks, St. Augustine, Florida.

Forry, Samuel
"Letters of Samuel Forry, Surgeon, U.S. Army, 1837-1838"; Florida Historical Quarterly, Part I, VI, (Jan. 1928), 133-148; Part II, VI (Apr. 1928), 206-219; Part III, VII, (July 1928), 88-105.

Francke, Jr., Arthur E.
   1977, <u>Fort Mellon, 1837-42: A Microcosm of the Second Seminole War</u>, Banyan Books, Miami.
   1986, <u>Coacoochee, Made of the Sands of Florida, An Account of a Once-Free Seminole Chief Presented in Free Verse</u>, E.O. Painter Printing Company, DeLeon Springs, Florida.

1989, Secondary Scenarios of the Second Seminole War, n.p.

General James Jackson Chapter, D.A.R.
1942, History of Lowndes County, Georgia, 1825-1941, Valdosta, Georgia

Gibson, Lillian Dillard
1978, 1558-1978, Annals of Volusia, Birthplace of Volusia County, printed and published by R.
Alex Gibson at Volusia, Florida.

Gonzalez, Thomas A.
1932, The Caloosahatchee, Miscellaneous Writings Concerning the History of the Caloosahatchee River and the City of Fort Myers, Florida, Koreshan Unity Press, Fort Myers, Florida.

Gray, James M.
1978, Forts of Florida, Florida Historical Research Foundation.

Grismer, Karl H.
1950, Tampa, A History of the City of Tampa and the Tampa Bay Region of Florida, St.
Petersburg Printing Co., Inc., Florida.

Gulf Archaeology Research Institute (GARI)
1999, The Nature Coast and Its Cultural Environment, Volume III: Notes on The Seminole Wars, Crystal River, Florida.

Hanna, Alfred Jackson
1936, <u>Fort Maitland, Its Origin and History</u>, The Rollins Press, Winter Park, Florida.

Hanna, Alfred Jackson, and Hanna, Kathryn Abbey
1948, <u>Lake Okeechobee, Wellspring of the Everglades</u>, The Bobbs-Merrill Company Publishers, Indianapolis & New York.

Heatherington, Alma
1980, <u>The River of the Long Water</u>, The Mickler House Publishers, Chuluota, Florida.

Heidler, David S., and Heidler, Jeanne T.
1996, <u>Old Hickory's War, Andrew Jackson and the Quest for Empire</u>, Stackpole Books, Mechanicsburg, PA.

Heitman, Francis B.
1903, <u>Historical Register and Dictionary of the United States Army... to March 2, 1903</u>, 2 Vols., Government Printing Office.

Hughes, Kenneth J.
1992, <u>A Chronological History of Fort Jupiter and U.S. Military Operations in the Loxahatchee Region, 1838-1858</u>, Florida Coast Research and Publishing Inc., Fort Lauderdale.

Hutchison, Ira A.

Some Who Passed This Way, (No publication page. History of Bay County and St. Andrew area.)

Hutchinson, Janet, and Paige, Emeline K.
1987, History of Martin County, Florida Classics Library, Port Salerno, Florida.

Huxford, Folks
1948, The History of Brooks County, Georgia, Hannah Clarke Chapter, D.A.R., Quitman, Georgia.

"Jacksonville and the Seminole War, 1835-36"; Florida Historical Quarterly, Part I, Vol. III, (Jan.
1925), 10-14. Part II, Vol. III, (Apr. 1925), 15-21. Part III, Vol. IV, (Jul. 1925), 22-30.

Kimball, Christopher D.
2001, Timeline of Events and Battles of the Florida Seminole Wars, self-published.

Kimber, Edward
1744, A Relation, or Journal, of a late Expedition to the Gates of St. Augustine, On Florida, part of the Floridiana Facsimile Series, University Press of Florida, Gainesville, 1976.

Kinnaird, Lawrence, and Kinnaird, Lucia B. War Comes to San Marcos, Florida Historical Quarterly, LXII, (Jul. 1983), 25-43.

Knetsch, Joe

A Second Ending: Broward in the Indian Scare of 1849, Broward Legacy, Vol. 11, Num. 3, (Summer/Fall 1988) pp. 22-24.

The Range Wars Move South: The Seminole Wars as a Continuations in the Conflict Over Cattle and Land, The Proceedings of the Florida Cattle Frontier Symposium, 1845-1995, Florida Cattlemen's Association and the Florida Cracker Cattle Breeders Association, 1995, Kissimmee, Florida, pp. 54-63.

"Airy and Comfortable" Or Live in the Forts During the Second Seminole War, Apalachee, Vol. XI (1996) Tallahassee Historical Society, pp. 25-35.

Jesup's Strategy, the Founding of Fort Lauderdale and the Role of Lieutenant Colonel James Bankhead, Broward Legacy, Vol. 19, Num. 1-2, (Winter/Spring 1996) pp. 19-24.

"All His Wants Should Be Promptly Supplied": Persifor F. Smith and the Caloosahatchee River Campaign of 1837-1838, The Sunland Tribune, Journal of the Tampa Historical Society, Vol. XXII (November 1996) pp. 19-26.

Benjamin A. Putnam, The Battle of Dunlawton – Part 1, Halifax Historical Society, Halifax Herald, Vol. 16, Num. 2, (December 1998) pp. 1-5.

William Cooley and the Beginnings of the Homosassa Settlement, At Home, Citrus County Historical Society, Vol. 16,

Num. 1 and 2, (Jan/Feb and Mar/Apr 1999).

    Southeast Florida in the Third Seminole War: Roads, Scouts and Expeditions, Part I, Broward Legacy, Vol. 22, Num. 1-2, (Summer/Fall 1999) pp. 38-45.

    Into the Cove Again: Worth's 1841 Campaign, At Home, Citrus County Historical Society, Vol. 16, Num. 6, (Nov/Dec 1999).

    2003, Florida's Seminole Wars, 1817-1858, The Making of America Series, Arcadia Publishing.

Knight, Lucian Lamar
1913, Georgia's Landmarks, Memorials and Legends, The Byrd Printing Company, Atlanta, Georgia

Lamme, Robert E.
1975, Third Seminole War Military Map of South Florida as Ordered by the Hon. Jefferson Davis Secretary of War U.S.A., with Overlay of Present Day Roads and Cities, Hialeah, Florida.

Laumer, Frank
    This Was Fort Dade, Florida Historical Quarterly, XLV, (Jul. 1966), 1-11.

    1968, Massacre!, University of Florida Press, Gainesville, Florida.

    1995, Dade's Last Command, University Press of Florida, Gainesville.

1998, <u>Amidst A Storm of Bullets, 1836-1842, The Diary of Lt. Henry Prince in Florida</u>, University of Tampa Press, Tampa.

Litrico, Helen Gordon (Not mentioned on the title page, but believed to be this author.)
1973, <u>Amelia Island Explored: Facts, Fables, Findings... Fishing and Sightseeing Guides,</u> Amelia Island Plantation, Florida.

Mahon, John K.
   The Journal of A.B. Meek and the Second Seminole War, 1836, Florida Historical Quarterly, XXXVIII, (Apr. 1960), 302-318.
   1985, <u>History of the Second Seminole War 1835-1842</u>, Revised Edition, University Press of Florida, Gainesville, Florida.

Marotti, Jr., Frank
Edward M. Wanton and the Settling of Micanopy, Florida Historical Quarterly, LXXIII, (Apr.
1995) 456-477.

Martin, Joel W.
1991, <u>Sacred Revolt, The Muskogees' Struggle for a New World</u>, Beacon Press, Boston.

Matthews, Janet Snyder
1985, <u>Sarasota, Journey to Centennial</u>, Continental Heritage Press, Tulsa, Oklahoma.

McAlister, Lyle N.
William Augustus Bowles and the State of Muskogee, Florida Historical Quarterly, XL (Apr.
1962), 317-328.

McCall, George A.
1868, Letters from the Frontiers, part of the Floridiana Facsimile Series, University Presses of Florida, Gainesville, 1974.

McDuffee, Lillie B.
1933, The Lures of Manatee, Manatee, Florida.

McGoun, Bill
1972, A Biographic History of Broward County, The Miami Herald, Florida.

McIver, Stuart B.
1983, Fort Lauderdale and Broward County, An Illustrated History, Published by Windsor, Woodland Hills, California.
   1994, Dreamers, Schemers and Scalawags, The Florida Chronicles, Volume 1, Pineapple Press, Inc., Sarasota, Florida.

McKinnon, John L.
1968, The History of Walton County, Kallman Publishing Company, Gainesville, Florida.

McReynolds, Edwin C.

1985, The Seminoles, 4th printing, University of Oklahoma Press, Norman.

Melton, Faye Perry
1987, "Memories of Fort McCoy", Typeworld Printing & Typesetting, Ocala, Florida.

Melton Jr., Holmes
1976, Lafayette County History and Heritage, An Anthology, Special Bicentennial Edition.
(Reprints of local newspaper articles.)
Mayo Rotary Club, Mayo, Florida.

Missall, John, and Missall, Mary Lou
2004, The Seminole Wars, America's Longest Indian Conflict, University Press of Florida.

Moore, William V.
1858, Indian Wars of the United States, Jas. B. Smith & Co., Philadelphia.

Morris, Jerry C., and Hough, Jeffrey A., 2009, The Fort King Road: Then and Now, The Seminole Wars Foundation, Inc.

Motte, Jacob Rhett
1963, Journey into Wilderness, edited by James F. Sunderman, University of Florida Press, Gainesville.

1819, Narrative of a Voyage to the Spanish Main in the Ship "Two Friends", part of the

Floridiana Facsimile Series, University Press of Florida, Gainesville, 1978.

Neff, Jacob K.
1845, The Army and Navy of America, J.H. Pearsol & Co., Philadelphia.

Neill, Wilfred T.
1956, The Story of Florida's Seminole Indians, Great Outdoors Publishing Company, St. Petersburg, Florida.
Surveyors' Field Notes as a Source of Historical Information, Florida Historical Quarterly, XXXIV, (Apr. 1956) 329-333.

The News, St. Augustine
"Notes on the Passage Across the Everglades", Tequesta, XX, (1960) 57-65.

Opdyke, John B.
1974, Alachua County, A Sesquicentennial Tribute, The Alachua County Historical Commission, Florida.

Ott, Eloise R.
Fort King: A Brief History, Florida Historical Quarterly, XLVI, (July 1967) 29-38.

Ott, Eloise Robinson and Chazal, Louis Hickman
1966, Ocali Country, Kingdom of the Sun, A History of Marion County, Florida, Perry Printing Company, Ocala, Florida.

Patrick, Rembert W.
1954, <u>Florida Fiasco, Rampant Rebels on the Georgia-Florida Border, 1810-1815</u>, University of Georgia Press, Athens, Georgia.

Phelps, John W.
"Letters of Lieutenant John Phelps, U.S.A., 1837-1838, Florida Historical Quarterly, VI, (Oct.
1927), 67-84.

Pickett, Albert James
1988, <u>History of Alabama and Incidentally of Georgia and Mississippi from the Earliest Period</u>, the Reprint Company Publishers, Spartanburg, S.C.

Pizzo, Anthony P.
1968, <u>Tampa Town, 1824-1886, The Cracker Village With A Latin Accent</u>, Hurricane House Publishers, Inc., Miami.

Pope, John
1792, <u>A Tour Through the Southern & Western Territories of the United States of North-America</u>, part of the Floridiana Facsimile Series, University Press of Florida, Gainesville,
1979

Porter, Kenneth W.

Seminole Flight from Fort Marion, Florida Historical Quarterly, XXII, (Jan. 1944), 113-133.

The Episode of Osceola's Wife, Fact or Fiction?, Florida Historical Quarterly, XXVI, (July 1947), 92-98.

1996, <u>The Black Seminoles, History of a Freedom-Seeking People</u>, revised and edited by Alcione M. Amos and Thomas P. Senter, University Press of Florida, Gainesville.

Potter, Woodburne
1836, <u>The War in Florida</u>, reprinted under the March of America Facsimile Series, Number 77, University Microfilms, Inc., Ann Arbor, Michigan, 1966.

Procyk, Richard J.
1999, <u>Guns Across the Loxahatchee, an Archaeohistorical Investigation of Seminole War Sites in Florida, with a special focus on the Battle of Loxahatchee, January 24, 1838</u>, The Florida Historical Society.

Reavis, L. U.
1878, <u>The Life and Military Services of William Selby Harney</u>, Ryan, Brand & Co. Publishers, St. Louis.

Robinson, Jim, and Andrews, Mark
1995, <u>Flashbacks, The Story of Central Florida's Past</u>, The Orange County Historical Society and Orlando Sentinel, Orlando.

Rodenbough, Theo F.
1875, <u>From Everglade to Canon with the Second Dragoons (Second United States Cavalry)</u>, D. Van Nostrand, New York

Rucker, Brian R.
   West Florida's Creek Indian Crisis of 1837, Florida Historical Quarterly, LXIX (Jan. 1991), 315-334.
   In the Shadow of Jackson: Uriah Blue's Expedition into West Florida, Florida Historical Quarterly, LXXIII, (Jan. 1995), 325-338.

Sangster, Dess L., and Sangster, Tom
1993, <u>Fort Mims and the Tensaw Settlement</u>, Lavender Publishing, Bay Minette, Alabama.

Schene, Michael G.
1976, "The Georgia Volunteers and Fort Cooper", Bureau of Historic Sites and Properties, Bulletin No. 5, Division of Archives, History, and Records Management, Florida Department of State, Tallahassee.

Seley Jr., Ray B.
Lieutenant Hartsuff and the Banana Plants, Tequesta, Vol. XXIII (1963), 3-14.

Sewall, R.K.

1848, <u>Sketches of St. Augustine</u>, part of the Floridiana Facsimile Series, University Press of Florida, Gainesville, 1976.

Sheldon, R.S.
Seminole Attacks Near New Smyrna, 1835-1856, Florida Historical Quarterly, VIII, (Apr. 1930) 188-196.

Simmons, William Hayne
1822, <u>Notices of East Florida</u>, part of the Floridiana Facsimile Series, University Press of Florida, Gainesville, 1973.

Sprague, Joseph T.
1848, <u>The Origin, Progress, and Conclusion of the Florida War</u>, part of the Floridiana Facsimile Series, University Press of Florida, Gainesville, 1964.

Steele, Willard
1987, <u>The Battle of Okeechobee</u>, Archaeological and Historical Conservancy, Florida Heritage Press, Miami.

Strickland, Alice
1985, <u>Ashes On The Wind, The Story of the Lost Plantations</u>, The Volusia County Historical Commission.

Sturtevant, William C.
Chakaika and the "Spanish Indians", Tequesta, # XIII, 1953, 35-74.

Swanton, John R.
1922, Early History of the Creek Indians and Their Neighbors, 1998 reprint by University Press of Florida, Gainesville.

Suarez, Annette McDonald; and Williford, William Bailey
1982, A Source Book on the Early History of Cuthbert and Randolph County, Georgia, Cherokee Publishing Company, Atlanta, Georgia

Sutton, Leora M.
1991, Success Beyond Expectations, Panton Leslie Co. at Pensacola, Vowell's Printing Company, Pensacola, Florida.

Tebeau, Charlton W.
    1955, The Story of the Chokoloskee Bay Country, with the Reminiscences of Pioneer C.S. 'Ted' Smallwood, University of Miami Press, Florida.
    1957, Florida's Last Frontier, The History of Collier County, University of Miami Press, Florida.
    1980, A History of Florida, 7th printing, University of Miami Press, Coral Gables, Florida.

Tillis, James Dallas
Original Narratives of Indian Attacks in Florida, An Indian Attack of 1856 on the Home of Willoughby Tillis, Florida Historical Quarterly, VIII, (Apr. 1930) 179-187.

United States Congress
1972, <u>The New American State Papers, Indian Affairs</u>, edited by Loring B. Priest, Scholarly Resources, Wilmington, Delaware.
1979, <u>The New American State Papers, Military Affairs</u>, edited by Benjamin Franklin Cooling, Scholarly Resources, Wilmington, Delaware.

United States Congress (24th Congress, 2d Session), January 23, 1837
<u>Report from the Secretary of War, In Compliance with Resolution of the Senate of the 14th and 18th Instant, Transmitting Copies of Correspondence Relative to the Campaign in Florida.</u>

Valliere, Kenneth L.
The Creek War of 1836, A Military History, The Chronicles of Oklahoma, Vol. LVII, Winter 1979-1980, pp. 463-485.

Van Doren, Mark, (edited by)
1928, <u>Travels of William Bartram</u>, reprinted in 1955 by Dover Publications, Inc., New York, N.Y.

Verrill, Ruth
1976, <u>Romantic and Historic Levy County</u>, Storter Printing Company, Gainesville, Florida.

Walker, Anne Kendrick

1941, <u>Backtracking in Barbour County, A Narrative of the Last Alabama Frontier</u>, The Dietz Press, Richmond, Virginia.

Waselkov, Gregory A.
2006, <u>A Conquering Spirit, Fort Mims and the Redstick War of 1813-1814</u>. The University of Alabama Press.

Weisman, Brent Richards
   1989, <u>Like Beads on a String</u>, University of Alabama Press, Tuscaloosa.
   1999, <u>Unconquered People, Florida's Seminole and Miccosukee Indians</u>, University Press of Florida, Gainesville.

Welch, Andrew
1841, <u>A Narrative of the Early Days and Remembrances of Osceola Nikkanochee, Prince of Econchatti, Written by his Guardian</u>, part of the Floridiana Facsimile Series, University Press of Florida, Gainesville, 1977. Introduction and indexes by Frank Laumer.

White, Jr., Frank F.
   A Journal of Lt. Robert C. Buchanan during the Seminole War, The Battle of Lake Okeechobee, Florida Historical Quarterly, XXIX, (Oct. 1950) 132-151.
   A Scouting Expedition along Lake Panasoffkee, Florida Historical Quarterly, XXXI, (Apr. 1953) 282-289.

White, Jr., Frank L.
The Journals of Lieutenant John Pickell, 1836-1837, Florida Historical Quarterly, XXXVIII, (Oct. 1959) 142-171.

Wickman, Patricia R.
1991, Osceola's Legacy, The University of Alabama Press, Tuscaloosa and London.

Williams, John Lee
1827, A View of West Florida, part of the Floridiana Facsimile Series, University Press of Florida,
Gainesville, 1976

Winsberg, Morton D.
1988, Florida's History through Its Places: Properties in the National Register of Historic Places, Institute of Science and Public Affairs, Tallahassee, Florida.

Wolf, John B.
1989, The Battle at the Loxahatchee River: The Seminole War, Loxahatchee Historical Society, Jupiter, Florida.

Woodward, A.L.
Indian Massacre in Gadsden County, The Florida Historical Quarterly, I, (April 1908), pp. 17-25.

Woodward, Thomas S.
1859, Woodward's Reminiscences of the Creek or Muscogee Indians, contained in letters to friends in Georgia and Alabama,

by Thomas S. Woodward, of Louisiana (formerly of Alabama) With an appendix containing interesting matter relating to the general subject., Barrett & Wimbish, Montgomery, Alabama. From internet web page by Jim Upchurch, www.mont.mindspring.com/~jtu3/wood/contents.html

Worsley, Etta Blanchard
1951, Columbus on the Chattahoochee, Columbus Office Supply Company, Columbus, Georgia.

Wright, Jr., J. Leitch
   1967, William Augustus Bowles, Director General of the Creek Nation, University of Georgia Press, Athens, Georgia.
   1986, Creeks and Seminoles, University of Nebraska Press, Lincoln and London.

Young, Julia J.
A Tallahassee Alarm of 1836, Florida Historical Quarterly, VIII, (Apr. 1930) 197-199.

Young, Rogers W.
Fort Marion During the Seminole War 1835-1842, Florida Historical Quarterly, XIII, (Apr. 1935), 193-223.

Made in the USA
Columbia, SC
31 January 2018